classic & contemporary

CHRISTMAS CAKES

classic & contemporary

CHRISTMAS CAKES

Nadene Hurst

with Julie Springall

MEREHURST

Contents

Introduction

Christmas is one of the most important festivals of the year.
For the cake decorator, it provides numerous ideas and
subjects to choose from, as well as the perfect opportunity
to experiment with colour, shape and materials.
These cakes cater for a broad spectrum of tastes, from the
traditional to the modern, and bring a fresh approach to
design, colour and medium. For many people, Christmas may
be the only occasion when they make a special cake for their
families. Some of the cakes shown here are simple and quick to
make, yet are effective through their use of colour and design –
this is important at such a busy time of year and ensures you can
produce an artistic creation to grace your festive table.

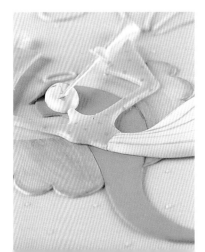

Christmas cracker surprise

This elegant, royal iced cake is decorated with piping and ribbons, and makes an attractive base for the elaborate Christmas cracker.

Cake and decoration

20cm (8in) square fruit cake

Apricot jam (jelly)

1kg (2lb/6 cups) marzipan

28cm (11in) square cake board

1kg (2lb/6⅔ cups) royal icing

Liquid cream food colouring [MF]

125g (4oz) pastillage (see page 97)

Icing (confectioners') sugar, for dusting

Edible glue

125g (4oz/¾ cup) white sugarpaste (rolled fondant)

125g (4oz) white flower paste

Lemon gold dusting powder (petal dust) [EA]

Painting solution [EA] or clear alcohol

3 metres (3⅓yd) 15mm (⅝in) wide gold satin ribbon

1 metre (1⅛yd) 15mm (⅝in) wide gold organza ribbon

2 metres (2¼yd) 23mm (⅞in) wide gold organza ribbon

Special equipment

5mm (¼in) spacers

Solid glue stick

No. 3 piping tube (tip)

4cm (1½in) diameter cardboard tube

Ribbed rolling pin [PME]

9cm and 8cm (3½ and 3in) round fluted cutters

Veining tool [HP]

Round piece of foam

1 Brush the top of the cake with apricot jam (jelly). Roll out half the marzipan between the spacers. Place the cake upside down on it. If the edge of the cake is sloped and there is a gap, fill it in with a roll of marzipan. Trim and smooth the edge of the marzipan level with the cake.

2 Leaving the cake upside down, cut four marzipan rectangles to fit the sides, adding 1cm (½in) to the length and 5mm (¼in) to the height. Brush the sides of the cake with the jam. Lift the marzipan pieces against the sides, with the bottom edge flat on the worktop and a side edge level with a corner of the cake, so that each corner has an overlap. Trim the excess level with the side of the cake to form sharp right angles. Push the marzipan that overlaps the top on to the base of the cake. Turn the cake the right way up on to the cake board and leave to dry.

3 Colour the royal icing cream and apply three coats to the top and sides of the cake. Coat the board with a soft consistency icing, then leave to dry.

4 Score across the top of the cake in both directions dividing it into four squares. Continue scoring down the sides and across the board to the edge. Measure along the lines to

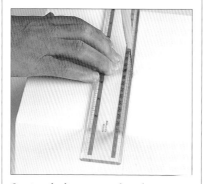

Scoring the lines across the cake

calculate the length of ribbon required, allowing an extra 2.5cm (1in). Cut two lengths of satin ribbon and overlay with equal lengths of organza. Seal together with dabs of glue stick. Attach to the cake, over the scored lines, with a line of royal icing. Bend the ends down on to the side edge of the board and glue.

Overlaying the ribbon and attaching it

5 Working on one corner, measure along the top and bottom edges of the cake between the corner and the ribbons in the centre of both sides, and mark at 1cm (½in) intervals. Score vertical lines down the sides of the cake joining the marks. (To make them clear, the scored lines are shown in pencil in the pictures.)

6 With a No. 3 tube (tip), pipe rows of pearls to cover the lines and down the corner edge. Repeat this process on the diagonally opposite corner.

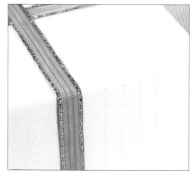

Marking the vertical lines onto the cake

Piping over the vertical lines and down the corner

7 To decorate the remaining two corner sections, place a ruler from the top corner point to the bottom edge against the ribbon and score a line. Measure and score lines parallel to this, 1cm (½in) apart. Repeat this on both sides of the corner. Pipe along these lines as before.

8 Finish off the top and bottom edges of the cake with another row of pearls using the No. 3 tube.

9 Start the cracker by making a pastillage tube. You will need a 4cm (1½in) diameter tube (the one used here was from the inside of a kitchen paper (towel) roll). Roll out the pastillage and cut an oblong piece

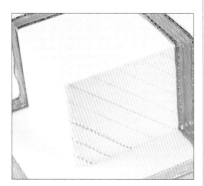

Marking and piping the diagonal lines

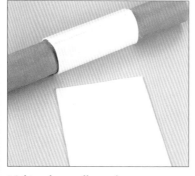

Making the pastillage tube

11cm (4½in) wide and slightly longer than the circumference. Dust the pastillage with icing (confectioners') sugar to prevent it from sticking and place it around the tube. Overlap at the join and fasten with edible glue. Leave to dry for about 24 hours, or until the paste is really hard. Slide the pastillage tube off the cardboard roll.

10 Mix together the sugarpaste (rolled fondant) and flower paste, then colour cream to match the cake. Roll out and texture by rolling with the ribbed rolling pin. Cut out an oblong, 13cm (5in) wide and long enough to fit around the pastillage tube. Make sure that the ribbed lines will run along the length of the cracker.

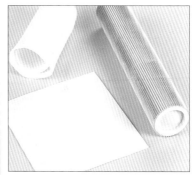

Stages of covering the tube with paste

11 Place the piece of paste around the tube of pastillage and secure underneath with edible glue. Brush the overhanging paste at the ends with glue and tuck them around the pastillage on to the inside of the tube.

12 Roll out the remaining paste and cut out two 9cm (3½in) fluted circles. Frill around the edges using a veining tool, which will also add texture, to a depth of at least 2.5cm (1in). Soften down some paste with edible glue and spread it around the ends of the tube to attach the circular frills. You will need this extra strong glue, as the weight of the frills can pull them away from the edge of the tube. Push the frills backwards on to the tube while you make two more similar ones. Stick these inside the first ones and place a round piece of foam or a cutter against each end. Draw the frills over to rest on them until dry.

13 Remove the supports from the frills. Make two 8cm (3in) frills and push these inside the dry ones. Pull the frilled edges together to hide the

Tucking in the excess paste

Stages of making the first two frill layers and drying over a support

Detail of the finished bow

centres. Leave to dry completely, then paint the edges of all the frills with lemon gold dusting powder (petal dust) mixed with painting solution or clear alcohol.

14 To make the bow for the centre of the Christmas cracker, wind a length of gold satin ribbon into two loops 13cm (5in) long. Tie the loops together around the centre with narrower ribbon, pull the loops apart and twist them inside out. Trim the tails. Using the wider gold organza ribbon, wind six loops 13cm (5in) long. Tie them in the centre and pull apart the loops, twisting each one to keep them separated in the same way as the satin bow. Turn three or four of the loops inside out to make them stand up. Tie this bow on to the top of the satin one.

15 Place a satin ribbon overlaid with organza, the same as on the cake, around the centre of the cracker. Attach the cracker diagonally to the top of the cake, where the two ribbons cross in the centre. Finish by sticking on the bow with royal icing, and attaching satin ribbon to the edge of the board.

Detail showing the end of the cracker

Helpful hints

• Royal iced cakes can be stained by moisture from the cake migrating under the marzipan. Pushing the excess marzipan on to the base creates a seal with the cake board and prevents this from happening.
• Paddle the icing thoroughly before placing it in the piping bag to prevent air bubbles from spoiling the appearance of the piping.
• Before using a ribbed rolling pin, sprinkle the surface of the paste with extra icing (confectioners') sugar and rub it into the surface. This will help to prevent the rolling pin from sticking.

Stages of making the bow for the centre of the Christmas cracker

Winter lace

A stacked two-tier Christmas cake makes an unusual and eye-catching centrepiece. Pale blue icing and lacy white Christmas trees combine in elegant simplicity.

Cake and decoration

20cm (8in) and 13cm (5in) square fruit cakes

Apricot jam (jelly)

1.5kg (3lb/9 cups) marzipan

28cm (11in) square cake board

13cm (5in) square cake card

Clear alcohol

1.5kg (3lb/9¾ cups) baby blue sugarpaste (rolled fondant) [R]

500g (1lb/3 cups) royal icing

Gum tragacanth (optional)

Silver snow dusting powder (petal dust)

Painting solution [EA]

25g (1oz) white flower paste

1.5 metres (1⅝yd) 3mm (⅛in) wide silver ribbon

1 metre (1⅛yd) 39mm (1½in) wide silver organza ribbon

Silver ribbon for the edge of the board

Special equipment

Bobble tool [HP]

No. 2 piping tube (tip)

Run-out film

Templates (see page 106)

Scriber

1cm and 2cm (½in and ¾in) star cutters

1 Brush the cakes with apricot jam (jelly) and cover with marzipan. Put the base cake on the board and the smaller one on the cake card. Brush with alcohol. Roll out the sugarpaste (rolled fondant) to 5mm (¼in) and cover the cakes.

2 When the sugarpaste on both cakes is dry, position the small cake on top of the base towards one corner, about 2.5cm (1in) from the edges on two sides. Leave the cake card in position under the cake, as this will prevent the moisture in the cake from softening the sugarpaste underneath, making it easier to remove later. A small amount of royal icing under the card will prevent the cake from moving.

3 Roll out the remaining sugarpaste and cut four strips to cover the board. Mitre at the corners, rubbing over the joins to blend the edges together. Using a bobble tool, press into the paste over a join, from the point on the corner of the board to the corner of the cake, and rock sideways slightly to impress with the bobbles. Continue along the board in the same manner, at intervals of 2.5cm (1in), keeping the impressions parallel to the one on the first corner of the board.

Stop when you reach the second corner of the cake. Repeat the

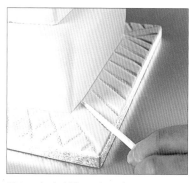

Using the bobble tool on the sugarpaste

process in the opposite direction, starting with a line on the second corner. Finish all the sides of the board in the same way, then fill in the gaps on the corners with shorter parallel lines as shown. Leave the sugarpaste to dry.

4 Soften some of the royal icing with boiled water. Paddle it to a piping consistency and place in a piping bag with a No. 2 tube (tip). Pipe a line around the base of both tiers to attach the narrow silver ribbon.

Attaching a ribbon around the cake base

5 Cover a flat board with thin run-out film, securing it with masking tape at the corners. Trace the pattern for the side cake trees and place underneath the run-out film (see overleaf). The pattern can be carefully moved along, as required, to pipe the necessary number of pieces. You will need 20 of these trees, but it is useful to pipe a few extra ones, as they are very delicate, and can break during handling.

Paddle some royal icing, adding a pinch of gum tragacanth to strengthen the piped pieces. Feed it into a piping bag with a No. 2 tube. Paddling the icing first helps to prevent the lines from breaking – this is because air bubbles pop as they come out of the tip of the tube and can make the piping brittle.

6 Commence piping the trees with the top branches. Start at the curl on one side, pipe inwards and upwards to the centre. Overlap slightly as you bring the line down again and finish with the curl on the opposite side. By piping each set of branches with one line, the finished piece will be much neater. Continue down the tree in the same manner, making sure that the lines touch on the outsides, where the lines curl, and in the centre. These joins are very important, as the whole cake will collapse if they are not strong enough.

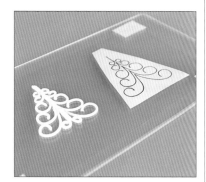

Piped section of a tree

7 When the trees are dry, paint them with silver dusting powder (petal dust) mixed with painting solution or clear alcohol. Do not let the painting solution become very wet or it will weaken the icing.

8 To remove the trees from the film, cut around each one with a scalpel, leaving a margin of film, turn over and peel the film off the back. You can do this on the palm of your hand or on a piece of foam.

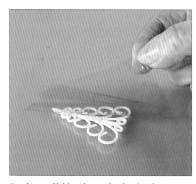

Peeling off film from the back of a tree

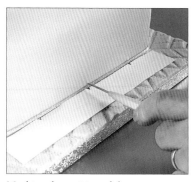

Marking the position of the trees

9 Trace and cut out the side templates. Place them flat against the side of the cake, and mark the position of the centre of each tree with a scriber. Remove the templates, pipe a line of icing down the back of each tree, and attach them to the sides of the cakes.

Supporting the tree sections with foam

10 Pipe the standing tree pieces in the same way – there are three sizes and for each one you will need a double piece and two half sections. Dry, peel off the film and paint on both sides. Pipe a line down the centre of the double section and attach a half piece at a right angle. Support with foam until dry.

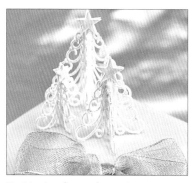

Positioning the top decoration

11 Stand the tree up and attach the remaining half piece section at a right angle, as before. Paint over the joins when they are dry.

Thinly roll out the flower paste and cut out two small, and four larger, stars. Paint with the silver solution. Attach the stars to the top of each tree, on both sides, to cover the joins.

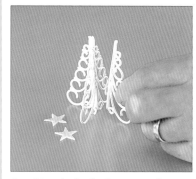

Attaching the final side to a standing tree

12 Using silver organza ribbon, tie a double bow in the centre of a metre (1⅛yd) length. Attach this to the front corner of the top tier and allow the tails to fall down to the edge of the base cake board. Stick the tails to the edge of the board and trim. Cover the edge of the board with a silver ribbon, covering over the end of the tails.

Attaching ribbon to the edge of the board

Carefully position the standing trees on top of the cake behind the bow.

Helpful hint

Attach the trees and bow with softened blue sugarpaste so that the joins will be less noticeable.

Crown of holly

Capturing the very essence of Christmas, this realistic display of holly leaves and bright red berries crowns a smartly panelled cake in shades of lemon and lime.

Cake and decoration

2 x 18cm (7in) round fruit cakes, each 5cm (2in) deep
Apricot jam (jelly)
750g (1½lb/5 cups) marzipan
18cm (7in) round thin cake board
1kg (2lb/6½ cups) sugarpaste (rolled fondant)
Lime green, lemon, Christmas green, holly green [S] and red paste food colourings
Clear alcohol
25cm (10in) spare cake board
Edible glue
300g (10oz) flower paste
Vegetable fat, for greasing
Cornflour (cornstarch), for dusting
Icing (confectioners') sugar, for dusting
Green and brown dusting powder (petal dust)
26 and 28 gauge green covered wires
Edible varnish

Special equipment

Pizza or mini cutting wheel [PME]
Small stitch wheel [PME]
Templates (see page 106)
Grooved non-stick board [C]
Firm foam pad
Veining tool [J]
Large ball tool [J]
Pimple foam
Airbrush (optional)

1 To make up the depth of the cake, sandwich together the two round cakes. Brush the top of one cake with apricot jam (jelly), place a disc of marzipan on top, brush again with jam and place the second cake on top of the marzipan. Treat the stacked cakes as a single one.

2 Place the cake on the thin cake board. (This will remain under the cake after the decoration is finished, so that it can be presented without a cake board showing.)

3 Marzipan the cake. Colour 750g (1½lb/5 cups) sugarpaste (rolled fondant) lime green and roll out to 5mm (¼in) thick. Brush the marzipan with clear alcohol and cover with the sugarpaste. This will hide the board underneath. Leave for 24 hours to dry.

4 Place the cake on the spare board. Cut out an 18cm (7in) round template, fold into eight and place on top of the cake. Divide the edge into eight with a scriber at each point of the template. Place a ruler down the side of the cake, in line with each point, and scribe a line down to the board.

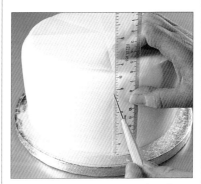

Scribing the eight lines down the side

5 Measure the width and height of each panel, add 2.5cm (1in) to the height and make a template.

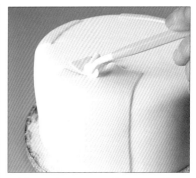

Adding and trimming a lemon panel

Add some lemon colouring to half of the remaining green sugarpaste. Roll out thinly and cut out four pieces, using the template. Brush edible glue down the sides and across the bottom, then stick on to the side of the cake over alternate panels. Press the top edge over on to the top of the cake. Trim in a semi-circle, using a cutting wheel.

Attaching the white strips

6 Measure around the base of the cake. Mix together 125g (4oz) white sugarpaste and flower paste and roll out a length 33cm (13in) long and 2.5mm (⅛in) thick. Using a ruler and stitch wheel, mark two straight lines 1cm (½in) apart. Cut out the strip leaving a small margin on the outside of these stitches. Brush the back with edible glue and place around the bottom edge of the cake. Repeat to complete the circle.

7 Roll out the white paste again, and cut matching strips 13cm (5in) long. Attach these vertically to the side of the cake, covering the joins between the panels, continuing them over the top edge of the cake. Leave to dry.

Cutting out the leaf using a template

8 Colour about 60g (2oz/⅓ cup) flower paste with Christmas green food colouring and about 60g (2oz/⅓ cup) with holly green food colouring. Make a template of the holly leaf shape, unless you have a cutter of the same size and a similar shape.

Lightly smear the area of board around the groove with vegetable fat. Roll out a small amount of flower paste over the groove and cut out the leaf using the template.

9 Pick up the leaf and insert a piece of 26 gauge wire into the base, pushing it half way up the length.

Turn the leaf right side up on to a firm foam pad dusted with a mixture of cornflour (cornstarch) and icing (confectioners') sugar, and mark in the veins with a veining tool.

Veining and shaping the holly leaves

10 Turn the leaf over again and rub along the edges with a ball tool to stretch them and create a curled effect. Drape the leaf over pimple foam to dry and avoid flattening out. You will need to make a minimum of 50 holly leaves.

11 Add highlights to the holly leaves by brushing with dusting powder (petal dust) or airbrushing. Add some green around the edges, and a little brown on the tips. Pass through a jet of steam.

12 Colour the remaining flower paste red. Make the berries by rolling small pieces into balls. Place one berry on the palm of your hand and insert a 28 gauge wire through the centre; push until you can feel the wire touch your hand. This will make a tiny realistic bump on the top surface of the berry. Leave to dry. Varnish and leave to dry again.

Taping the berries into bunches

13 Group at least seven berries together in a bunch and fasten with tape 2.5cm (1in) below the berries. Continue the taping along the length of the wires, adding one leaf at a time, until a circle of five leaves surrounds the berries, then wind the tape down to the end of the wires. You will need at least ten of these bunches.

14 Using a ball of the remaining lime green sugarpaste, make a flat disc for the top of the cake, 2.5cm (1in) deep and 5cm (2in) in diameter. Brush one side with edible glue and place in the centre of the top of the cake.

15 Trim the stems on the back of the bunches of holly and insert them into the side of the disc of sugarpaste on top of the cake to form a continuous ring. Arrange them so that the tips of the holly leaves are just overhanging the edge of the cake. Fill the hole in the centre by inserting more bunches into the top of the disc. Check all around the cake and rearrange the leaves to cover any spaces. Ten bunches should be enough, but if there are any large gaps, you will need to use more.

Inserting the holly bunches into the disc

16 Carefully remove the cake from the temporary cake board, but keep the cake card in place. Place it on a cake stand to take pride of place on your Christmas tea table.

Helpful hints

• A small cutting wheel is easier and quicker to use than a knife for cutting out the holly leaves, and will not drag the flower paste.
• If the dusting mixture contains icing (confectioners') sugar, you will achieve a better shine on the leaves when steamed.
• Smear a small amount of vegetable fat on your hands before rolling the berries and inserting the wires to prevent them from sticking.

New England Christmas

The covering of this cake is a kind of edible paint effect with its aged, crackle glaze look. The garland of dried oranges, cloves and cinnamon sticks adds to the traditional feel.

Cake and decoration

20cm (8in) round fruit cake

Apricot jam (jelly)

1kg (2lb/6 cups) marzipan

1kg (2lb/6½ cups) white sugarpaste (rolled fondant)

Cream, autumn leaf, chestnut, paprika, dark brown, tangerine, Christmas red, liquorice black, holly green and claret paste food colourings [S]

28cm (11in) round cake board

225g (7oz) modelling paste

45g (1½oz) flower paste

Skin-tone, red, brown, black and shadow grey dusting powders (petal dust) [S]

Piece of raffia

1 tablespoon royal icing

Superwhite powder

50cm (20in) red gingham ribbon

1.5 metres (2yd) white ribbon for the edge of the board

Special equipment

Nos. 10 bristle and 1 and 4 sable paintbrushes

Pair of compasses

Star cutter, smallest from set of 3 [FMM]

Nos. 0, 1.5, 2, 3 piping tubes (tips) [PME]

5-star cone tool [J]

Veiner R9 [OP]

Holly cutters H2 and H3 [OP]

Dimple foam

Template (see page 104)

Veining tool

Size 1 bow cutter [J]

Glass-headed pin

1 Brush the cake top with apricot jam (jelly). Roll out the marzipan and cover the top, then the sides of the cake.

2 Knead 900g (1lb 13oz/5¾ cups) sugarpaste (rolled fondant) and mix in a little of the cream food colouring. Roll it out and cover the cake. Save the trimmings, re-knead and roll out into a long strip to cover the board. Leave to set overnight.

3 Mix a little autumn leaf food colouring on a tile with water using the No. 10 bristle brush. Take off some of the excess colour from the brush on some kitchen paper (towel).

Brushing the cream colour over the cake

4 Brush the colour on to the cake, rolling the side of the bristles back and forth. Then brush the board. Paint criss-cross lines with a No. 1 brush and chestnut colouring and water.

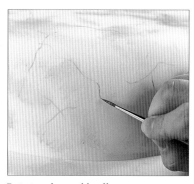

Painting the crackle effect

5 With the compasses, draw a 13cm (5in) circle on a piece of greaseproof (wax baking) paper. Leave a 4cm (1½in) gap all the way around and cut out. Place on a spare cake board, secured with masking tape. Colour 120g (4oz) modelling paste with the same cream food colouring as the cake covering. Divide into two and roll one half out into a sausage about 58cm (23in) long. Cover with cling film (plastic wrap) and roll out the remaining half into another sausage. Brush a little water down one side, place the first sausage next to it and twist them together along the length to make a garland.

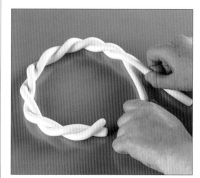

Twisting the modelling paste garland

6 Lay the twisted garland on the board, following the circle on the paper. Trim off the excess paste at the top, making a neat join. Leave to dry overnight before moving.

Leaving the garland to dry in shape

Cutting out and piercing the centres of at least five star buttons

Drying the holly leaves on dimple foam

7 Colour 10g (⅓oz) of flower paste terracotta using paprika and dark brown food colouring. Roll out and cut out five stars, plus a few spares, with the star cutter. Cut two little holes from the centre of each star using the tip of the No. 1.5 piping tube (tip). Leave to dry on a spare board.

8 To make the cinnamon sticks, colour 20g (¾oz) modelling paste a cinnamon colour using autumn leaf, paprika and a touch of dark brown food colourings. Roll out into a strip and trim to 3cm (1¼in) wide. Trim the top, paint water across the width and roll over once, then trim across the bottom edge with a sharp knife. Make five, plus spares, and leave to dry. Dust with skin-tone dusting powder (petal dust), then tie a small piece of raffia around each stick.

Rolling and tying the cinnamon sticks

9 For the oranges, colour 30g (1oz) modelling paste with tangerine, Christmas red and dark brown. Set aside 7g (¼oz). Divide the rest into six equal portions and roll into balls. Mark about seven holes in the top of each one with the 5-star cone tool, then roll on the finest side of a grater.

Dust with a little red and brown dusting powder with a dry No. 4 brush. Mix some black food colouring

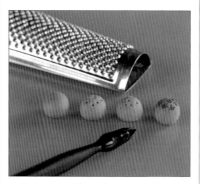

Imitating the effect of orange peel

into a teaspoon of royal icing and fill a bag fitted with a No. 0 piping tube. Pipe four small lines around each hole to look like cloves.

10 For the holly, colour 10g (⅓oz) flower paste a mid-green colour with holly green and black, and another 10g (⅓oz) a darker shade of green with the same colours. Roll out the

mid-green colour and press the veiner all over the surface. Place the holly cutter (H2) over one impression so it is lined up centrally and press down firmly. Ball lightly around the edges without distorting the shape. Leave to dry on dimple foam. Make 10 x H2, and 10 x H3 mid-green leaves and 12 x H2, and 8 x H3 darker green leaves. When they are dry, dust a few of them with a tiny amount of black dusting powder.

11 Roll out 35g (1¼oz) modelling paste into a thin strip long enough to fit around the cake. Trim along one long side and two short sides. Then cut a wavy line on the remaining long

Cutting the beaks and feet of the geese

side so the strip is roughly 15mm (⅝in) deep. Moisten the base of the cake and wrap around the strip, making a neat join. Run the tip of your finger along the wavy edge to soften the line. Leave the snow border to set.

12 Measure the circumference of the cake with a tape measure. Divide into six and mark off this point just above

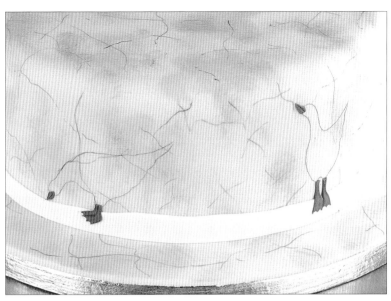

Sticking the beaks and feet to the corresponding goose on the side of the cake

the snow with a pencil dot. Trace the three geese from the template and cut into separate tracings, turn over, then trace on the back. Transfer two of each goose outline to the sides of the cake above the pencil dots. Roll out the reserved orange modelling paste and transfer the beaks and feet tracings (two of each). To do this, lay the tracing on the paste (pencil side down) and rub over it (just the area you

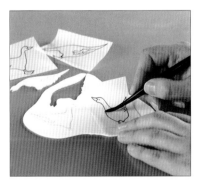

Transferring the tracing of a goose

need) with a veining tool. Remove, then cut out the beaks and feet with a sharp knife. Stick the beaks and feet to the outlines on the cake with water. Mark a line across their beaks and between their legs.

13 Roll out 10g (⅓oz) of white modelling paste and transfer all three geese on to the surface of the paste

as for the feet and beaks. Cut around the outlines and stick to the corresponding feet on the cake. Smooth the edges with a finger. Mark the wings with a veining tool. Repeat with another three geese and the remaining paste. Dust the wings with a little shadow grey using a dry No. 1 brush, then paint in the finer details and eyes with black food colouring and a No. 1 brush.

14 For the bows around the necks of the geese, colour 10g (⅓oz) flower paste a beige colour with a little dark brown food colouring. Roll out the paste thinly and cut out six sets of bows with the size 1 bow cutter. Paint a line of water around the geese's necks and attach the long ties, trimming neatly. Dot some water in the middle of the bow and fold the two

Cutting out the bows for the necks

ends into the centre. Lay the bow over the small square of paste and wrap around the middle so all the joins are at the back. Stick to the necks of the geese on the sides of the cake and leave to dry. Paint in the lines to look like gingham using claret and dark brown food colourings mixed with superwhite and water. Use a No. 1 sable paintbrush.

15 Mix the remaining royal icing with some cream food colouring to match the covering and fill a bag fitted with a No. 2 tube. Carefully turn over the garland twist and pipe a little icing on the back. Turn the right way and stick to the top of the cake so that the join is at the top. Press down gently and remove any icing which may have oozed out with a damp paintbrush.

16 Tie a large bow with the wide gingham ribbon. Pipe a blob of icing at the top of the garland over the join, stick the bow over the icing and insert a glass-headed pin to hold it in place. When dry, remove the pin.

17 Build up the arrangement starting with the sprigs of holly. Colour the remaining flower paste with claret and dark brown and roll tiny balls for the berries. Secure them in the centre of the sprigs of holly with a little dot of water. Make tiny holes in the berries with a pin. Using royal icing, attach the oranges, cinnamon sticks and star buttons, filling in any gaps with more holly and berries. Finally, secure a length of white ribbon around the board using a glue stick.

Helpful hints

• If you do not have a grater, roll the oranges over the top of an upturned metal sieve instead.
• You may find it helpful to use the tip of a No. 3 piping tube (tip) to help cut the shape of the geese's webbed feet.

Midnight snowflakes

The infinite geometric patterns of snowflakes are the inspiration for this attractive cake. Set against the dark blue sugarpaste, they produce a really spectacular effect.

Cake and decoration

23 x 13cm (9 x 7in) oval fruit cake

Apricot jam (jelly)

1kg (2lb/6 cups) marzipan

30 x 25cm (12 x 10in) oval cake board

Clear alcohol

1kg (2lb/6½ cups) dark blue sugarpaste (rolled fondant)

Icing (confectioners') sugar, for dusting

500g (1lb/3⅓ cups) royal icing

1 metres (2¼y) dark blue velvet ribbon for the edge of the board

Special equipment

Run-out film

Templates (see page 104)

Nos. 0, 1 and 2 piping tubes (tips)

Scriber

1 Brush the cake with apricot jam (jelly) and cover with a layer of marzipan. Place the cake on the board, brush with clear alcohol and cover with dark blue sugarpaste (rolled fondant). Dark coloured pastes are easily spoiled by patches of icing (confectioners') sugar. Use only a small amount when rolling out, and avoid using it on the top surface if possible. If it is needed to prevent the top surface from sticking, sprinkle it over the paste and rub in with the palm of your hand before rolling. When the cake is covered, polish the surface with your hand.

Outlining and filling in a snowflake

2 Brush the exposed area of the board with water. Roll out the remaining paste into two long lengths about 5cm (2in) wide and cover the board, overlapping the join. Cut through both thicknesses and remove the excess. To disguise

Pricking the pattern on the cake

the join, pinch the paste together and rub over it with your finger, then press with a smoother. Trim around the edge with a sharp knife. Leave to dry.

3 Cover a flat board with run-out film. Trace the snowflake templates. Place the pattern of the largest snowflake under the film. Outline the run-sugar areas with a No. 0 piping tube (tip). Fill in with a thick consistency run-sugar, starting with the centre, and place under the heat of a desk lamp to dry.

Place the pattern for the large snowflake on one end of the top of the cake, with one of the straight

Piping the soft graduated bulbs

run-sugar lines running vertically. Prick through the pattern with a pin to mark the positions of the series of bulbs, then remove the pattern.

Put the dried piece of the large snowflake in position on the cake, alternating it with the lines of pricked holes. Attach it with small bulbs of royal icing.

4 Reduce some icing to a very soft piping consistency and place in a piping bag with a No. 1 tube. Pipe the series of graduated bulbs radiating from the centre of the pattern, applying less pressure as the bulbs get smaller. Place under a desk lamp to skin over and give them a shine.

Close-up of largest snowflake to show the added piping

Examples of piped snowflake patterns

5 Using a No. 1 piping tube, cover the centre of the large snowflake with small bulbs.

Pipe a line down the centre of each of the six run-sugar spurs, then pipe short lines radiating away from these centre ones in the same manner as veining on a leaf. Finally, overpipe the long, centre lines to neaten.

6 Some of the remaining snowflakes are based on a solid star shape or flower shape, each in different sizes for the centres.

Place these patterns under run-out film on a flat board, soften some icing to a thick run-sugar consistency and place in a piping bag without a tube. Pressure pipe these shapes, without an outline. For the stars, pipe a bulb in the centre and pull out the icing on to the points, using a paintbrush. For the flower shapes, pipe a bulb in the centre and one at the end of each petal, and brush in the area between. Dry under a lamp.

7 Use a large flower shape, and one large and one medium star shape as the centres of the three remaining snowflakes on top of the cake. Attach these to the cake and pipe in the remaining decoration for each snowflake, using a soft piping consistency in Nos. 0, 1 and 2 piping tubes.

8 Work down the side of the cake and pipe different sizes and patterns of snowflakes, starting with the larger

ones near the top edge. Use the run-sugar centres for them, and Nos. 0 and 1 tubes for the piping. A selection of various snowflake patterns is shown here, but you can experiment and make up more versions of your own. Remember that all snowflakes are based on six-sided figures.

Close-up of piping on board

9 Close to the bottom of the cake, pipe a few flakes without using any run-sugar pieces. This will enable you to pipe smaller ones which are useful to fill in any gaps. Use Nos. 0 and 1 piping tubes.

10 With the soft piping consistency again, almost cover the board with randomly piped bulbs to represent a sprinkling of snow. Use the No. 2 tube closest to the cake, working outwards with the No. 1 tube and then using the No. 0 on the outside. Do not pipe right up to the edge of the board all the way around it.

11 Finish the edge of the board with a length of dark blue velvet ribbon to match the sugarpaste.

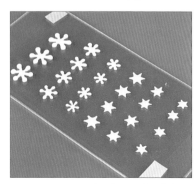

Run-sugar centres for the smaller flakes

Close-up of the top three smaller flakes

Christmas roses

The trefoil shape and green colour scheme of this cake make the perfect backdrop for the beautiful Christmas roses.

Cake and decoration

20cm (8in) trefoil-shaped cake

25cm (10in) round cake card

Apricot jam (jelly)

1kg (2lb/6 cups) marzipan

2 x 28cm (11in) round cake boards

Clear alcohol

1kg (2lb/6½ cups) pale green sugarpaste (rolled fondant)

Christmas green [S] and yellow paste food colourings

125g (4oz/¾ cup) white sugarpaste

250g (8oz) white flower paste

28 gauge green covered wire

Light green, yellow and fleshtone dusting powders (petal dust) [S]

Painting solution [EA]

Edible varnish [SK]

26 and 28 gauge white covered wires

White sewing cotton

Light green stemtex

Edible glue

Yellow Sugartex [SF]

1 metre (1⅛yd) 7mm (¼in) wide green satin ribbon

1 metre (1⅛yd) 15mm (⅝in) wide green satin ribbon

Special equipment

3mm (⅛in) spacers [SSS]

Petunia 435 and 599 cutters [TKT]

Glass-headed pins

Grooved rolling out board [C]

Large rose leaf cutter [SC]

Foam pad

Large ball tool [J]

Rose petal and rose leaf veiners

Christmas rose 284 cutter [TKT]

Soft sponge

1 Bake the cake in a trefoil tin (pan); the amount of mixture will be about the same as for an 18cm (7in) round cake. Draw around the baking tin and cut out the shape from the cake card, then place this under the cake.

2 Brush the cake with apricot jam (jelly). Roll out the marzipan and use to cover the cake. Place the cake on a cake board, with the cake card still underneath. Brush the marzipan with clear alcohol. Roll out the pale green sugarpaste (rolled fondant) and use to cover the cake. Trim and reserve the excess. Leave the cake to dry.

3 Set aside 60g (2oz/⅓ cup) of the remaining pale green sugarpaste. Colour the rest darker green. Roll it out between the spacers to ensure an even thickness across the paste, then cover the second cake board. Trim around the rim of the board, then cut out shapes around the edge at random using the petunia cutters.

Cutting out flower shapes on the board

4 Roll out the white sugarpaste between the spacers and cut out flowers with the same cutters. Remove the green flower shapes from the board and replace with white flowers. Rub the surface gently with a smoother to improve the join between the two colours of paste. Paint light

green stamens radiating from the centre of the flowers and add spots of yellow over the top of the green to complete the effect.

Leave to dry, then transfer the cake on to this board, still leaving the cake card underneath it.

Replacing the cut outs with white flowers

5 Attach the narrower green ribbon around the base of the cake with softened sugarpaste. Use glass-headed pins to hold it until dry, then remove.

6 Colour 90g (3oz) of flower paste pale green and roll into a small ball, using the grooved board. Turn the paste over and cut out a leaf with the ridge up the centre. Insert a 28 gauge green wire in the ridge for the full length of the leaf. Place on a firm foam pad and thin the edges with a ball tool. Position the leaf on a veiner and press sufficiently to lose the ridge

Making the flower paste leaves

down the centre. Bend the leaf, including the inserted wire, and twist the sides slightly to create a natural movement. Leave to dry.

7 When dry, brush the leaves with dark green dusting powder (petal dust) and tip the edges with fleshtone dusting powder. Pass them through a jet of steam to fix the colours, then varnish. You will need 33 leaves (one for each flower), three stems of three leaves, and six stems of two leaves, taped together.

8 To make the centres of the flowers, wrap a length of white cotton around two fingers 40 times. Slide it off your fingers, twist the coil in the centre and fold the two loops together. Push a 26 gauge white wire through the loops and twist tightly underneath. Trim the wire to 10cm (4in) long.

Making the centres of the flowers

9 Using one-third width light green stemtex, bind the wire, starting at the bottom and working up towards the loops. Finish by wrapping the stemtex tightly around the base of the cotton strands to hold them together.

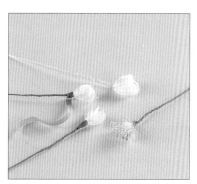

Binding stems and finishing stamens

Making the the Christmas rose petals

Cut through the top of the loops, and trim the stamens to 1cm (½in). Place on kitchen paper (towel) and brush with light green dusting powder.

Very gently brush the tips of the stamens with the side of a paintbrush, dipped in edible glue. Touch the tips on to yellow Sugartex to pick up the powder on the ends. Leave to dry.

10 Roll out a small piece of flower paste for each petal on the grooved board. Turn it over, cut out the petal and insert a 28 gauge white wire up through the centre ridge. Place the petal on a veiner and press firmly, making sure that the ridge is flattened and the edges are thinned. Place the petal on soft sponge and press in the centre with a large ball tool to create a cupped shape. Leave to dry. Brush inside the base of each with pale green dusting powder, then pass through a jet of steam to fix the colour.

11 To assemble, use half width stemtex and bind around the base of the stamens, adding one petal at a time. When five are in place, continue

Assembling the flowers

Placing the three-leaf stems first

taping for 2.5cm (1in) down the wire, then pull the ends of the petal wires to tighten the fit around the stamens. Add a leaf, and continue taping to the end of the wire. Make 12 stems.

12 Mould a dome of pale green sugarpaste and attach to the centre of the top of the cake. Insert the flower and leaf stems, starting with three-leaf stems resting on the indents of the cake. Follow with a ring of six flowers, another ring of five inside this and finish with one in the centre. Trim the length of the stems as you work along so that the flowers form a dome shape. Use the remaining six sets of two leaves to fill in any gaps.

Arranging the flowers and leaves

Helpful hint

To ensure that the colour scheme works well, purchase the ribbon before starting the cake. Then all the rest of the colours can be blended to match. This is because it will be more difficult to find ribbon that exactly matches the food colouring.

Christmas angels

The Christmas carol 'Hark! The Herald Angels Sing' is the inspiration for this cake. Angels are a traditional theme, but using pale turquoise, mauve, gold and silver gives the cake a contemporary look.

Cake and decoration

20cm (8in) hexagonal fruit cake
Apricot jam (jelly)
1kg (2lb/6 cups) marzipan
950g (2lb/6½ cups) white sugarpaste (rolled fondant)
Ice blue, grape violet, autumn leaf, chestnut, dark brown and black paste food colourings [S]
28cm (11in) hexagonal cake board
240g (7½oz/1¾ cups) royal icing without glycerine
60g (2oz) modelling paste
Superwhite powder
Silver [SK], cream and rose [S] dusting powders (petal dust)
Cornflour (cornstarch)
Dipping solution
Snowflake glitter
1.5 metres (1⅔yd) 3mm (⅛in) wide silver lamé ribbon
1.75 metres (2yd) ribbon for the edge of the board

Special equipment

Templates (see page 103)
Small star cutter
Nos. 0, 1 and 4 paintbrushes
Nos. 0, 1 and 1.5 piping tubes (tips)
Run-out film
Crank handled palette knife
Foam sponge

Cutting the gold stars with the star cutter

1 Brush the cake top with apricot jam (jelly). Roll out the marzipan and cover the top, then the sides.

2 Colour 800g (1lb 10oz/5 cups) sugarpaste (rolled fondant) mauve with ice blue and grape violet food colourings and cover the cake. Colour 150g (5oz/1 cup) sugarpaste pale gold with a tiny amount of autumn leaf food colouring. Roll it out into a long strip and cover the board making a neat join at the back. Leave to harden.

3 Photocopy the angels for the sides of the cake to give four templates (for three run-outs and one spare) and the large angel. Trace the wings, halos and hair, then transfer the small ones to alternate sides of the cake and the large one to the top (include the scrolls). Make a tracing of the angel's hand holding the trumpet. Secure silver lamé ribbon around the base with a blob of royal icing.

4 Colour 40g (1¼oz) modelling paste medium gold using autumn leaf food colouring. Roll out a little, reserving the remainder for the wings, and cut out about 15 stars with the small star cutter. Stick the stars to the remaining three sides of the cake with a little water. Paint small dots on the cake

Painting small blue dots on the cake

surface, avoiding the wings, hair and stars, using ice blue food colouring with a little superwhite powder and water and a No. 0 brush.

Transferring the angels' wings

5 Roll out the gold modelling paste. Rub over the tracing for the angels' wings and transfer four times. Cut around the pencil lines with a sharp knife, moisten the sides and top of the cake with water and stick the wings in position, lining up the edges with the marks. Rub over the cut edges with a finger to round them off. Colour 15g (½oz) modelling paste brown with chestnut food colouring and repeat the process as above for each angel's

Placing the wings and hair in position

hair. Leave to dry overnight. Shade the centre of each pair of wings and hair with a little dark brown food colouring, mixed with water, using a No. 4 brush, and blend evenly.

6 Colour 40g (1¼oz/⅓ cup) royal icing flesh colour with chestnut, 75g (2½oz/½ cup) gold with chestnut and autumn leaf, and 100g (3½oz/⅔ cup) pale turquoise with a little ice blue. Add a few drops of water to the flesh colour ready for pressure piping and fill a bag fitted with a No. 1 piping tube (tip). Tape a piece of run-out film to a board with the images of the side angels underneath. Pipe their necks. Leave to skin over under a desk lamp.

Pressure pipe the heads. Outline the skirt with a No. 0 tube in turquoise. Let down the rest of the icing to a run-out consistency and fill in the skirt using a No. 1.5 tube. Leave to skin over. Outline the music

Piping the angels for the sides of the cake

with a No. 0 tube with white icing and fill in with white run-out icing and a No. 1.5 tube. Pressure pipe the hands and leave to skin over. Pipe the body and sleeve outlines in gold with a No. 0 tube. Thin the rest of the icing and fill in using a No. 1.5 tube.

7 Tape a piece of run-out film to a board with the large angel image underneath. Pipe in the following order, letting each colour dry: neck, head (pressure pipe), the empty hand, feet, body and skirt. On a separate board, pipe the trumpet with white icing, which needs to be of pressure piping consistency. Use a No. 1 tube and begin with two lines piped from the hand to the mouthpiece into a point. Then, outline from the hand to the end of the trumpet and squeeze in icing to fill. Leave to dry. Pressure pipe the thumb in flesh colour with a No. 1

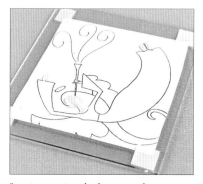
Starting to pipe the large angel

tube. When it has skinned over, pipe the fingers. When it is dry, paint the trumpet with silver dusting powder (petal dust) mixed with a little dipping solution, using a No. 0 brush.

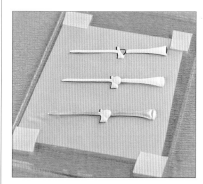
Stages of making the trumpet

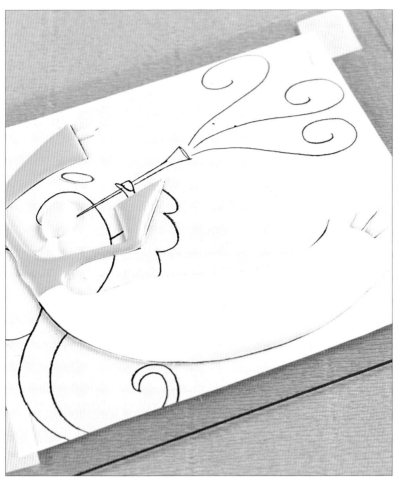

Piping the large angel, letting each colour dry before piping the next

8 Make sure the run-outs are dry before finishing. To finish the large angel, dust the waist and hem of the skirt and a few areas on the body with cream dusting powder and a No. 4 brush. Dust two small circles of rose and cream powder mixed with cornflour (cornstarch) for her cheeks using a No. 1 brush. Paint stripes on her skirt and dots on her body with cream dusting powder mixed with water using a No. 1 brush.

For the face, paint two small white circles for eyes, then pale turquoise, made with ice blue food colouring and water, just above the eye. Paint a nose with diluted dark brown and eyelashes, eyebrows and pupils with dark brown mixed with a little black. Paint a small heart with rose dusting powder and water for her mouth and paint a line across the middle with dark brown and black.

9 Finish the smaller angels in the same way. Shade the music with cream dusting powder and paint 'JOY' with a No. 0 brush and dark brown and black colouring mixed with a little water. Paint ovals for the mouths with dark brown and black and outline with rose dusting powder and water.

10 Mix a few drops of water into a teaspoon of royal icing and fill a bag fitted with a No. 0 tube. Pipe small dots on top of the turquoise dots painted earlier by touching the cake surface with the tip of the tube – it will leave behind the tiniest dot. When dry, paint the piped dot with silver dusting powder mixed with dipping solution. Colour about a teaspoon of royal icing with autumn leaf to match the angels' wings. Pipe in the scrolls on top of the cake with a No. 1.5 tube and the halos with a No. 1 tube.

11 Use a crank-handled palette knife (metal spatula) to slide under the small angel run-outs to loosen them from the run-out film. Flip them over on to foam sponge, one at a time, pipe a little icing on the back and gently stick to the sides of the cake over the wings and hair. Repeat for the large angel, piping larger bulbs of icing on the underneath of the lower part of her skirt. Line her up with the wings and hair and gently lower into place.

Loosen the trumpet and hand from the film. Flip over on to foam sponge and pipe a little icing at the base of the hand and a little way along from the mouthpiece. Stick in position on top of the cake with the mouthpiece near the angel's lips and so the hand is at the top of the sleeve. To finish, secure a length of ribbon around the board and sprinkle a little snowflake glitter on the board covering.

Positioning the trumpet

Helpful hint

To pressure pipe, squeeze bulbs of icing, letting it build up, then wiggle the tube in the icing and any ripples will disappear. Ease the icing into any awkward corners with the help of a damp No. 1 paintbrush.

Happy Christmas

A traditional theme and colours have been used for this attractive royal iced cake, which offers an opportunity to display your piping skills. All the decoration is edible.

Cake and decoration

20cm (8in) square fruit cake

Apricot jam (jelly)

1kg (2lb/6 cups) marzipan

20cm (8in) square thin hard cake board

1.25kg (2½lb/8⅓ cups) royal icing

Cream liquid food colouring [MF]

2 x 30cm (12in) square cake boards

Red, lime green, leaf green and brown paste food colourings

Lemon gold dusting powder (petal dust) [EA]

Gum tragacanth

Painting solution [EA] or clear alcohol

Gold ribbon for the edge of the board

Special equipment

Low-tack masking film

Nos. 0, 1, 1.5, 3, 42, 43 and 44 piping tubes (tips)

Templates (see page 104)

Run-out film

Crank-handled palette knife (metal spatula)

1 Brush the cake with apricot jam (jelly). Roll out the marzipan and coat the top and sides of the cake separately to form a sharp angle around the top edge. Place the cake on the thin cake board and leave to dry for 24 hours. The thin board will remain underneath the cake to protect the fully coated larger red board on which it is to be presented. Without this, the coated board would quickly be stained by the moisture from the cake and the underside of the cake would become unpleasantly sticky.

2 Colour the royal icing with cream liquid food colouring. Place the cake with the thin board underneath on to a spare cake board, and apply three layers of icing to the top and sides of the cake allowing each coat to dry before applying the next. This is a temporary board and care should be taken to clean up around the base of the cake after each side coating, or it will become difficult to remove the cake from the board later.

3 Colour 375g (12oz/2½ cups) of the remaining royal icing red. Coat the second cake board with three layers of icing. Trim carefully around the edges with a sharp knife or scalpel in between each coat. This will leave a lighter coloured mark on the surface; if you need to trim on the final coat, brush over any marks with a slightly damp paintbrush and the area will return to its original colour.

4 Cut strips of low-tack masking film 4cm (1½in) wide and attach them to the sides of the cake, level with the top edge, so that they are covering the top half of the sides. Overlap the pieces as you go around the cake, which will help to keep them in place.

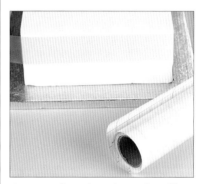

Cutting and attaching the masking film

5 Apply red icing around the base of the cake and smooth. Pull away the film to reveal a neat separation of the two colours. Leave to dry.

Smoothing red icing against the film

6 Score around the base of the cake with a scalpel. Carefully lift it off the spare board, keeping the thin board underneath, and place in the centre of the red-coated one. Pipe a border of small shells around the base in red using a No. 43 tube (tip). Then, pipe a second border around the top of the red coating on the side of the cake.

Piping the shell borders

Piping the main stem over the tracing on top of the cake

7 Trace the patterns for the piped scrolls and place on a flat board, under thin run-out film. Pipe with cream icing using a No. 3 tube. You will need eight of each pattern, but spares are a good idea. When they are dry, overpipe each one with a No. 1.5 tube down the centre of the No. 3 line. Paint the thinner line gold with gold dusting powder (petal dust) and painting solution or clear alcohol.

9 For the ferns, start at the base of each one and pipe short lines away from the centre stem, slanting up towards the tip. Gradually decrease the length of the lines to form a leaf shape. In some places, the ferns will overlap slightly, so you will need to allow the ones underneath to dry first. When you complete a piece of fern, overpipe down the centre stem to neaten the appearance.

Stages of making the leaves and cones

11 Make the cones separately on run-out film. Using the same green icing as the holly leaves, outline the oval shape and fill in with the run-sugar. Leave to dry under direct heat, then pipe tiny brown shells around the edge of each one using a No. 42 tube. Finish by piping another series of bulbs on the top, as shown, to create a domed shape.

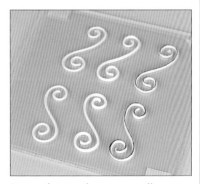

Stages of piping the corner scrolls

Piping a fern leaf

8 Trace the lettering and the main stem line of the top decoration on to a 20cm (8in) square piece of tracing paper, then transfer the design to the top of the cake. Using a No. 0 piping tube, pipe in the stems with lime green royal icing.

10 Make the holly leaves separately on run-out film. Outline each leaf with leaf green icing using a No. 1 tube, and pipe a centre stem. Fill in one side with run-sugar and leave under direct heat until crusted over, then fill in the remaining side. Leave to dry.

Helpful hint

Liquid colourings can be added with a glass dropper. Count the number of drops used to each 500g (1lb/3⅓ cups) icing, then the colour can be reproduced accurately when required.

Stages of making the bow

Detail showing the lettering

16 Pipe the lettering in the same green colour as the leaves, using a No. 1 tube. Attach the ribbon to the edge of the board.

Helpful hints

• When adding paste colour to royal icing, leave it as long as you can to mature, preferably overnight. The colour will darken, so take this into consideration when first adding the paste. In time, unmixed spots of colour will dissolve and be easily dispersed by beating the icing before use.

• Low tack masking film is used mainly for airbrushing; masking tape is a substitute, but do not press it on too firmly or you may spoil the surface.

• When painting a thin line of piping, load the brush heavily with the paint and then touch the line with just the side of the brush.

• If you own an airbrush, the edges of the holly can be sprayed in a darker green, and the top of the cones can be touched up with black.

• Never push backwards with the tube when piping shells. Only the tip of the previous shell should be covered, leaving the complete outline of each one showing.

12 To make the bow, outline the shapes in red icing, using a No. 1 tube. Fill in with run-sugar, working on the two parts separately in the sequence shown above, leaving each area to skin over under direct heat, such as a desk lamp. When completely dry, assemble the two pieces and pipe around the centre knot, adding lines radiating from it, as shown in the main picture.

14 Carefully remove four of each pattern of piped scrolls from the run-out film with a crank-handled palette knife (metal spatula). Arrange two scrolls on each corner of the board and attach them with small bulbs of royal icing in their centres. Make sure that the icing touches both the scrolls and the board, but handle the scrolls with care, as they are quite fragile and can break easily.

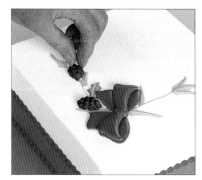

Assembling the top decoration

Detail of the scrolls on the cake and board

13 To complete the design on top of the cake, first place the bow in position at the base of the line of ferns. Attach it with small bulbs of royal icing. Then, add the holly leaves and, finally, the cones, attaching both with dots of royal icing.

15 Remove the remaining scrolls. Pipe shells around the top of the cake in cream-coloured icing, using a No. 44 tube. While still wet, attach two scrolls to each corner. Check their position before pushing them gently into the soft shells to secure.

Madonna and child

The Virgin Mary and baby Jesus appear in all manner of religious imagery, such as icons, statues and fine art. This is an apt image to choose for a cake to remind us of the meaning of Christmas.

Cake and decoration

20cm (8in) square fruit cake

Apricot jam (jelly)

15cm (6in) round and 28cm (11in) oval cake boards

Small amount of royal icing

1kg (2lb/6 cups) marzipan

750g (1½lb/7 cups) sugarpaste (rolled fondant)

Caramel/ivory, baby blue, ice blue, chestnut, dark brown and black paste food colourings

15g (½oz) pastillage (see page 97)

Lemon gold [EA] and rose and cream [SF] dusting powders (petal dust)

290g (10oz) modelling paste (ratio of one flower paste to two of sugarpaste)

Dipping solution

Sugar glue

Cornflour (cornstarch)

Superwhite powder

1.5 metres (2yd) gold ribbon for the edges of the boards

Small amount of raffia

Special equipment

Serrated knife

Templates (see page 105)

No. 0 piping tube (tip)

Nos. 0, 1 and 4 sable and No. 5 bristle paintbrushes

Veining tool

1 Shape the fruit cake by first measuring 11.5cm (4½in) along the top from the top left corner, and then 11.5cm (4½in) down from the corner along the left-hand side. Make two cuts right through the cake at these points, creating an 11.5cm (4½in) square of cake, two equal rectangles and one small rectangle. Cut a slice 2.5cm (1in) wide off one long side of the small rectangle.

Cutting the cake into pieces for shaping

2 Begin to stack the cake, spreading apricot jam (jelly) between the layers. Start with the square, then stack the two medium rectangles, one on top of the other, the small rectangle and, finally, the slice laid flat.

3 Roughly trim the cake into a cone shape using a sharp serrated knife. Do not worry if it looks rather uneven at this stage.

Trimming the stacked cake into a cone

Baby Jesus nestles in His mother's arms

4 Stick the cake to the 15cm (6in) round board with a little apricot jam and begin to fill in any gaps in the shape with sausages of marzipan. Use the round cake board as a guide to obtain a circular base, rolling sausages of marzipan to fill in. Spread a thin layer of apricot jam over the whole surface.

Roll out the remaining marzipan into a rectangular strip large enough to go around the cake and about 5mm (¼in) thick. Wrap the marzipan around the cake, carefully smoothing out any air bubbles, and make a neat join at the back. Stick the cake, using royal icing to the centre of the 28cm (11in) oval cake board. Leave the cake to harden for a few days.

5 Colour the sugarpaste (rolled fondant) a creamy colour, using the caramel/ivory food colouring. Roll out and use to cover the cake as described for marzipan above. Leave overnight.

6 Trace the halo designs from the template. Make the halos for the Madonna and child by colouring the pastillage with the caramel/ivory food colouring. Roll out to a thickness of 1–2mm (⅟₁₆–⅛in) and use the tracings to cut out one of each. Leave to dry, turning once (see overleaf).

Stages in making the halos

7 When the halos are dry, pipe rows of dots around the edges with royal icing coloured with caramel/ivory in a No. 0 tube (tip). Leave to dry. Paint with lemon gold dusting powder (petal dust) mixed with dipping solution.

Tracing the outline of the Madonna

8 Trace the Madonna and child design from the template and transfer the outline for the Madonna to the front of the cake. Colour 220g (7oz) modelling paste with a mix of baby blue and ice blue, and 30g (1oz) modelling paste with chestnut for a flesh colour. Roll out 100g (3½oz) of the blue paste to 4mm (⅛in) thick. Use the tracing to cut out the Madonna's body and skirt, making sure that the

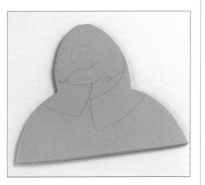

Transferring the lines for the child

lines for the child are also transferred. Stick to the marked area on the cake with sugar glue; soften the edges by rubbing with your fingers. Blend them flat to the surface and use your fingers to curve folds into her skirt.

Positioning the Madonna's body

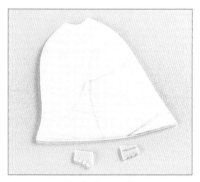

Cutting the child's feet and gown

9 Roll out 20g (¾oz) white modelling paste and cut out the child's gown. Cut out feet from a little flesh colour modelling paste. Stick on the feet and then the gown with sugar glue. Blend the edges where the Madonna's arms will overlap. Soften all the edges with your fingers. Stick the child's halo in place with royal icing and press lightly.

Positioning the feet, gown and halo

10 Roll out 20g (¾oz) flesh-colour modelling paste 1–2mm (¹⁄₁₆–⅛in) thick and cut out the Madonna's hands. Stick them in position with sugar glue. Roll out the remaining blue modelling paste to 3–4mm (⅛–¼in) thick and cut

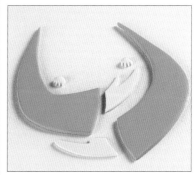

Cutting out the hands and arms

out the Madonna's arms. Stick them in position over her body and overlapping the body of the child, matching them up with the tops of her hands. Gently smooth the edges with your fingertip.

Roll two small balls, each one about 7mm (¾in) across, of flesh-colour modelling paste for the child's hands. Flatten one side. Cut small V-shapes out of the flat side to make four fingers. Stick the child's hands on top of the Madonna's arms.

11 Stick the Madonna's halo in place with a little cream royal icing. Roll out the remaining flesh colour paste to 3mm (⅛in) thick and use the tracing to cut out the Madonna's head and neck. Smooth the edges. Stick in place with sugar glue over the halo. Transfer the tracing for the child's head and, before cutting out, flatten the top so the paste is thinner there. Cut out and stick over the halo with sugar glue and soften the edges. Roll 20g (¾oz) white modelling paste into a sausage so it is 50.5cm (20in) long, fat in the middle and tapering at each end. Bend the ends around, into an oval shape. Stick around the Madonna's face with sugar glue and make a join at the top in the circle.

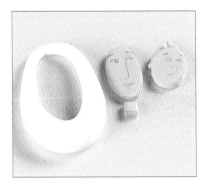

Cutting out the faces and hood

12 Dust the cheeks on both faces with a mix of rose and cream dusting powders and cornflour (cornstarch) with a No. 1 brush. Begin to paint in the features using a No. 0 brush. Paint superwhite on the whites of the eyes and ice blue irises. Use a pale

Stippling, then dusting the background to achieve a mottled effects

watery brown for their noses and the child's mouth and a mix of black and dark brown for the pupils, brows and lashes. Paint the Madonna's mouth with rose and cream dusting powders mixed with a little water.

13 Stipple the background of the cake with the caramel/ivory food colouring mixed with water using

Scattering raffia to resemble straw

the No. 5 bristle brush, so it is darker around the Madonna, and fading to a paler colour around the back. When the paint is tacky to the touch, dip the damp bristle brush into the lemon dust and stipple over the surface to achieve a mottled effect.

14 Attach a length of gold ribbon around the 15cm (6in) board. Roll out the remaining cream paste, left over from the covering, into a long strip and use to cover the board, making a neat join at the back.

15 Cut raffia into short lengths and scatter around the oval board. Trim the board edge with the remaining gold ribbon.

Helpful hint

The ideal depth of fruit cake is about 6cm (2½in) deep. If it is less than this, the stacked cake will not be tall enough and the template will be too big. Any deeper than this, and the cake will become too tall. Either way the template will need some adjustment.

Miniature cakes

Holly wreath

Cake and decoration

60g (2oz/⅓ cup) marzipan

Green paste food colouring

Brown and gold dusting powders (petal dust)

10cm (4in) round cake covered in marzipan and white sugarpaste (rolled fondant)

15cm (6in) round, thin gold cake board

60g (2oz/⅓ cup) red sugarpaste

Painting solution [EA]

Special equipment

Sugar shaper

6cm (2in) round cutter

Ribbed rolling pin [PME]

Large holly plunger cutter [PME]

1 Colour two-thirds of the marzipan green, soften with cool, boiled water and extrude through a sugar shaper with a trefoil-shaped fitting. Twist the length of marzipan and place around a 6cm (2½in) round cutter to support it. Leave to dry. Dust small areas of brown dusting powder (petal dust) at random around the circle and attach to the top of the cake.

2 Roll out the natural and green remaining marzipan. Press the colours together and roll out again. Cut out three holly leaves, twist and attach to the wreath. Roll and add three berries. Roll out the red sugarpaste (rolled fondant), impress with the ribbed rolling pin, and cut a 2.5cm (1in) ribbon for the base. Paint the leaf tips gold and brush along the wreath.

Stages of making the marzipan wreath

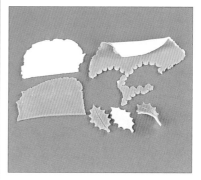

Making the two-tone holly leaves

Candle glow

Cake and decoration

Small amount of royal icing

10cm (4in) round cake covered in marzipan and ivory sugarpaste (rolled fondant)

15cm (6in) round, thin gold cake board

250g (8oz/1⅔ cups) red sugarpaste (rolled fondant)

Small amount of green flower paste

Small amount of yellow flower paste

Gold dusting powder (petal dust)

Painting solution [EA]

Edible varnish [SK]

5mm (¼in) green ribbon

Special equipment

Smoother

Glass-headed pin

Large holly plunger cutter [PME]

Medium ivy plunger cutter [PME]

Small rose petal cutter [TKT]

1 Pipe a line of royal icing around the base of the cake and attach the ribbon. Shape the red sugarpaste (rolled fondant) into a roll about 15mm (¾in) in diameter. Roll the paste backwards and forwards under a smoother with light pressure. Cut short lengths from the roll to the depth of the cake, then cut down the length of each one to make the half candles. Leave to dry.

Cutting out the half candles

2 Cut an 8.5cm (3½in) circle of greaseproof (wax baking) paper and fold into eight to make a template. Place on top of the cake. Attach the candles to the side of the cake using the template as a guide. Cut out four holly and ivy leaves from the green flower paste, twist and leave to dry for an hour on crumpled kitchen foil. Arrange these in a circle in the centre of the cake, and cover the join in the middle with red holly berries.

3 Cut out eight flames from the yellow flower paste with a small rose petal cutter. Leave to dry. Cut a small slit in the top of each candle with a scalpel. Slot a flame into each candle, using a small amount of royal icing to secure it. Paint the tips of the flames with gold dusting powder (petal dust) and paint the holly leaves and the candles with edible varnish.

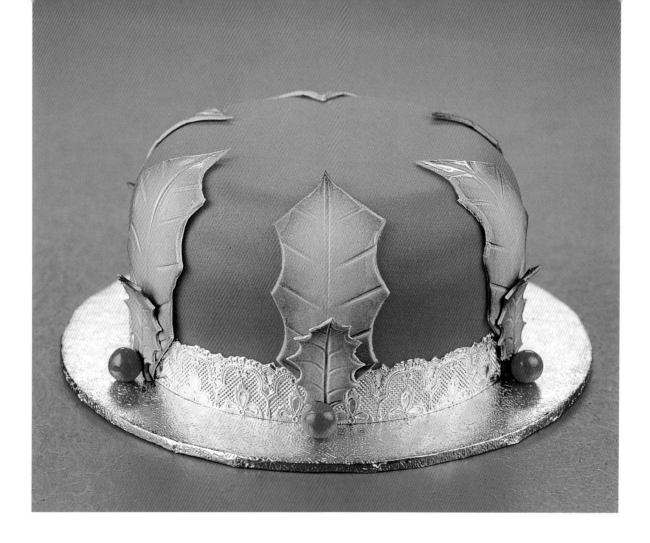

Winter berry

Cake and decoration

10cm (4in) round cake covered in marzipan and red sugarpaste (rolled fondant)

15cm (6in) round, thin gold cake board

60g (2oz) green flower paste

Dark green dusting powder (petal dust)

Edible glue

Small amount of red flower paste

Edible varnish [SK]

1cm (½in) wide gold paper ribbon

Special equipment

Template (see page 107)

Large holly plunger cutter [PME]

1 Cut out the template for the large holly leaves. Adjust the length to match the height of the cake, plus an extra 5mm (¼in). Attach the gold paper ribbon around the base of the cake (a paper ribbon will match the board). Cut out a 7.5cm (3in) diameter circle as a template. Fold into six sections and place on top of the cake. At the end of each fold, mark the surface of the cake to indicate the position of the holly leaves.

2 Cut out six holly leaves from the green flower paste. Mark the veining with the back of a knife. Dust the edges dark green and attach them to the sides of the cake with edible glue, bending the tips over the top. Cut out six small holly leaves and dust the back and edges dark green. Attach them to the larger leaves, bending the tips outwards. Roll six berries and place them at the base of the leaves. Varnish the leaves and berries.

Stages of making the holly leaves

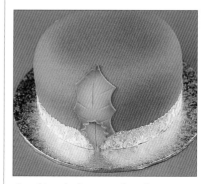

Attaching the leaves to the cake

Three crowns

Cake and decoration

60g (2oz/⅓ cup) red sugarpaste (rolled fondant)

60g (2oz/⅓ cup) blue sugarpaste

60g (2oz/⅓ cup) yellow sugarpaste

125g (4oz) white flower paste

10cm (4in) round cake covered in marzipan and ivory sugarpaste

Edible glue

15cm (6in) round, thin gold cake board

Green, orange and purple paste food colourings

Small amount of royal icing (optional)

Gold dusting powder (petal dust) [EA]

Painting solution [EA]

Special equipment

Frill cutters [PME and OP]

5.5cm (2¼in) and 8cm (3¼in) round cutters [CCS]

Small star, round and triangular cutters [CK]

No. 1 piping tube (tip)

1 Mix each coloured sugarpaste (rolled fondant) with 30g (1oz) flower paste. Roll out the red and cut out a strip with the large scalloped cutter. Trim the base straight to 2.5cm (1in) deep. Attach it to the base of the cake with edible glue. Roll out the blue paste and cut a strip, as shown, to a depth of 2.5cm (1in). Place the 8cm (3¼in) cutter on a flat board and wrap the strip around it. Gently bend out the tips to produce a curved effect. Leave to dry for 24 hours.

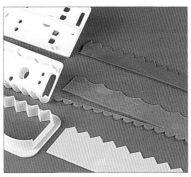

Frill cutters and the cut strips

2 Roll out the yellow paste and cut a strip, using the cutter shown, to a depth of 6cm (2½in). Place the 5.5cm (2¼in) round cutter on a flat board. Wrap the strip around it and gently bend the points so that they curve outwards. Leave to dry for 24 hours.

3 Colour the remaining flower paste and cut out some small shapes in green, orange, purple and yellow. If you do not have the shapes used here, use any small cutters. Stick these around the crown at the base of the cake and on the blue one. Place the yellow crown on top of the cake. Pipe pearls around the base using a No. 1 piping tube (tip). Use royal icing or softened sugarpaste. Slot the blue crown over the yellow one and finish off around the base in the same way. When the icing is dry, paint the piping around the blue crown with gold dusting powder (petal dust) and painting solution.

Blanket of snow

Cake and decoration

250g (8oz/1⅔ cups)
white sugarpaste (rolled fondant)

10cm (4cm) square cake
covered with marzipan and
pale turquoise sugarpaste

15cm (6in) thin, square
gold or silver cake board

Clear alcohol

30g (1oz) white flower paste

Special equipment

Star cutter [CK]

Small and large
Christmas tree cutters [TKT]

1 Roll out the sugarpaste (rolled fondant) to 3mm (⅛in) thickness. The piece will need to be at least 20cm (8in) wide and 15cm (6in) deep. Cut along the top edge in a random wavy line. Brush one half of the cake with clear alcohol, dividing the cake from corner to corner diagonally. Place the piece of white sugarpaste across the cake from corner to corner and smooth down the sides. Trim away the excess from the base and corners with a sharp knife.

2 Make a narrow roll from the remaining sugarpaste. Attach it to the base of the cake around the two uncovered sides and smooth the ends into the paste on the corners. Mix together the flower paste with an equal amount of sugarpaste and roll out thinly. Cut out a star, one large tree and two small trees. Attach the star to the corner of the cake, as shown. Place the trees along the edge of the snow line and trim away at the bases to fit against the curve.

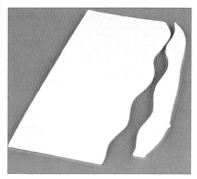

Cutting the white sugarpaste covering

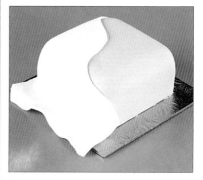

Draping the sugarpaste over the cake

Sparkling stars

Cake and decoration

60g (2oz/⅓ cup) white sugarpaste (rolled fondant)

60g (2oz) white flower paste

Edible glue

Granulated sugar

10cm (4in) square cake covered in marzipan and light blue sugarpaste

15cm (6in) thin, square gold or silver cake board

Small amount of royal icing

Special equipment

Templates (see page 107)

2.5cm (1in) triangular cutter [CCS]

No.1 piping tube (tip)

1 Trace and cut out templates for the star shapes. Mix together the white sugarpaste (rolled fondant) and flower paste. Roll out thinly and cut out the star shapes, using the templates. Leave them to dry. From the same paste, cut out one small star and 12 triangles. Leave to dry. Brush the surface of the stars and triangles with edible glue and sprinkle liberally with granulated sugar. Shake off the excess and leave to dry.

Sprinkling the stars with sugar

2 Attach two triangles at each corner with a bulb of icing. Place a triangle in the centre of each side and fill in the gaps with piped bulbs. Roll out the remaining paste to 5mm (¼in) thick and cut out a 2.5cm (1in) circle. Attach it to the centre of the top. Place the largest star on top, lining the points up with the corners of the cake. Stick on the medium star, alternating the points with the first one. Stand the smallest star on top.

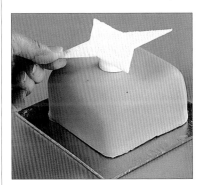

Placing the first star on top of the cake

Patchwork present

A colourful, fun Christmas present cake design, this is actually quite a straightforward cake for a beginner or intermediate cake decorator to create.

Cake and decoration

25 x 15cm (10 x 6in) fruit cake
Apricot jam (jelly)
800g (1lb 10oz/5⅓ cups) marzipan
25 x 35cm (10 x 14in) cake board
1kg (2lb/6½ cups) white sugarpaste (rolled fondant)
410g (13oz) modelling paste
Claret, tangerine, ice blue, gooseberry, melon and holly green paste food colourings [SF]
White vegetable fat
2 teaspoons royal icing
Silver dusting powder (petal dust) [SK]
Painting solution
150g (5oz) flower paste
Sugar glue
1.5 metres (2yd) of silver lamé ribbon for the edge of the board

Special equipment

2 bamboo skewers
Small Christmas tree cutter [PME]
Nos. 0 and 2 piping tubes (tips)
No. 0 paintbrush
Taffeta rolling pin [HP]

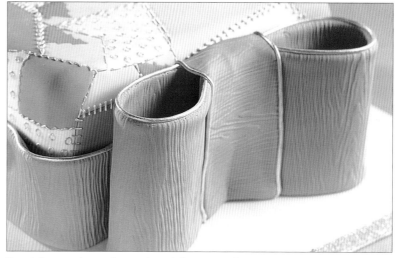

Detail showing the raspberry-coloured flower paste bow

1 Brush the cake with apricot jam (jelly). Roll out the marzipan and cover the top and side of the cake. Place the cake on the board. Cover the cake with 800g (1lb 10oz/5¼ cups) white sugarpaste (rolled fondant). Roll out the trimmings with the remaining sugarpaste into a long strip and cover the board. Leave overnight to harden.

2 Colour 100g (3½oz) of modelling paste with each of the following colourings: claret to make a raspberry colour, tangerine to make orange and a mixture of ice blue and gooseberry to make turquoise. Colour 10g (⅓oz) of paste with melon and holly to make a mid-green colour.

3 Roll out the modelling paste, one colour at a time, using the bamboo skewers as spacers to obtain an even depth of paste. Cut the paste into geometric shapes. Roll out more colours, including the remaining white modelling paste, and cut into geometric shapes as before.

4 To create the tree pattern on the turquoise colour, roll out the turquoise paste, using the spacers, and cover with cling film (plastic wrap) to prevent it from drying out. Roll out the green paste quite thinly on a thin film of white fat. Cut out some trees with the Christmas tree cutter, brush the backs with a little water and stick them randomly over the turquoise paste.

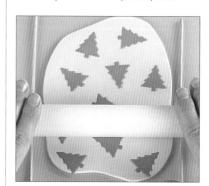

Rolling out the tree-decorated paste

5 Roll out the turquoise paste again, using the spacers – the trees will blend in. Cut the tree-decorated turquoise paste into geometrical shapes.

6 Gradually stick the coloured shapes randomly over the surface of the cake with water. Try not to get too many of the same colour next to each other.

To fill in the small gaps, press a piece of rolled paste over the gap, press, then remove. Cut out around the impression and insert in the gap.

Placing the coloured shapes at random

7 Fill a bag fitted with a No. 0 tube (tip) with royal icing. Pipe over the joins with various 'stitches', such as running stitch, herringbone, zig-zag, scallops and overstitching. Pipe small circles on the white paste shapes. Leave to dry.

Piping the 'stitches' along the joins

8 Paint the piping silver using a No. 0 brush, with a mixture of silver dusting powder (petal dust) and painting solution.

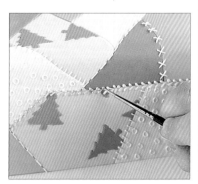

Painting the 'stitching' silver

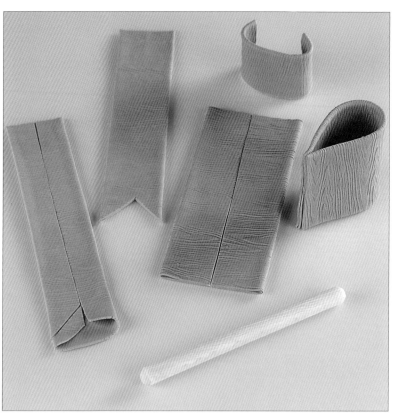

Making the bow and ribbon ties for the present

9 For the bow, colour the flower paste a shade of raspberry with the claret colouring to match the sugarpaste used on the cake. Roll out a quarter of the paste into a large rectangle about 3mm (⅛in) thick on a lightly greased surface. Roll over the surface with the taffeta rolling pin and trim to 15cm (6in) across and 17cm (6¾in) long. Turn the paste over, paint a line of water down the middle and fold the long edges into the middle. Paint water along the two short edges, curve the paste over and stick the short edges together, then stand it on its side. This will be a ribbon loop; repeat to make one more.

10 For the ribbon ties, roll out half the remaining paste into a rectangle longer than before and then roll over it with the taffeta rolling pin. Trim the paste rectangle to 9cm (3½in) across and 21.5cm (8½in) long. Flip the paste over, paint a line of water down the centre and fold the long edges into the middle.

11 To assemble the bow, cut a V-shape out of one short edge, then immediately lift and place on the board, around the top of the cake, so that the join is at the back. Secure in place with sugar glue. Repeat for the other tie. Paint sugar glue on the undersides of the ribbon loops and fix to the board over the ends of the ribbon ties. For the knot, roll out the remaining paste, roll over it with the taffeta rolling pin and trim to 9cm (3½in) across and 11cm (4½in) long. Flip over, paint a line of water down the middle and fold the long edges to the middle. Turn to the right side and stick on the place where the ribbon loops join in the middle, folding the edges under.

12 Pipe lines along the edges of the ribbon ties and bow, and on each side of the knot, with a No. 2 piping tube and white royal icing. When dry, paint silver with silver dusting powder mixed with painting solution. Glue a length of silver lamé ribbon to the board edge.

Festive marzipan wreath

This Christmas cake is decorated completely with marzipan and a wreath of marzipan fruits

Cake and decoration

20cm (8in) round fruit cake

25cm (10in) round gold cake board

Apricot jam (jelly)

1kg (2lb/6 cups) marzipan

Icing (confectioners') sugar

White vegetable fat or Tinslip (optional)

250g (8oz/1½ cups) modelling marzipan [R]

Dark green, lime green, brown, orange, yellow and red paste food colourings

Green and brown dusting powders (petal dust)

Edible varnish [SK] (optional)

Small amount of royal icing

1.5 metres (1⅔yd) wired edge organza ribbon (optional)

Special equipment

Closed curve crimper [PME]

Non-stick small rolling pin and board

Large plunger holly cutter [PME]

Dimple foam

Airbrush (optional)

5-star cone tool [J]

Plain cone tool [J]

Large ball tool [J]

Mini star cutter [PME]

Glass-headed pins (optional)

1 Place the cake on the board and brush with apricot jam (jelly). Roll out the marzipan and use to cover the cake. Make sure there are no creases around the base and polish the surface with your hand.

Crimping around the base of the cake

2 Crimp around the base of the cake with a serrated, closed curve crimper. If the crimper sticks, smear on a tiny amount of vegetable fat or Tinslip.

3 Colour 60g (2oz/⅓ cup) modelling marzipan dark green and 30g (1oz) lime green for the holly leaves. Work in extra icing (confectioners') sugar until the marzipan is no longer sticky to the touch.

Roll out a small amount of each colour, using a non-stick rolling pin. Do not dust with icing sugar. Keep picking up the marzipan as you are rolling out, to prevent it from sticking.

Cutting out and shaping the holly leaves

Cut out the holly leaves and impress the veins, using a plunger cutter. Twist the leaves slightly and place on dimple foam to prevent them from flattening out. Leave to dry.

4 When the leaves are dry and firm, colour them, using either an airbrush or dusting powders (petal dust). Touch the edges of the darker green leaves with brown. Add some green and a tiny amount of brown to the lime green leaves, and a little brown or green to the natural coloured ones.

Airbrushing will add a sheen to the surface, but dusting powders dull, so you may wish to brush the leaves with a little edible varnish. Allow the leaves to dry completely.

Drying the holly leaves on foam

5 Each fruit requires about 10g (⅓oz) modelling marzipan. Colour a small amount of marzipan brown for the stalks of the fruits.

6 To make, the oranges, colour 30g (1oz) marzipan orange and divide it into three equal portions.

Roll them into ball shapes and then roll lightly over the surface of a metal sieve for the orange-peel effect. Press a small, flattened piece of brown marzipan on the top, and indent using a star cone tool. If you are using an airbrush, the oranges will be enhanced

Marking the orange and lemon peel

if they are sprayed with orange colour. There is no point in dusting on extra colour, but an application of edible varnish will provide a sheen.

7 For the lemons, colour 20g (¾oz) marzipan yellow and divide into two equal portions.

Roll the two portions of marzipan into balls and then into egg shapes. Narrow them at either end and insert a cone tool in one end for a stalk hole. Roll the lemons lightly on the surface of the metal sieve to texture the peel in the same way as the oranges. Add a small amount of green colour on the tip opposite the stalk, then varnish, if necessary.

8 Colour 20g (¾oz) marzipan light green for the green apples. Use the same amount of natural marzipan colour for the red apples. Divide each colour into two equal portions.

Roll each into a ball shape and indent the top with a large ball tool. Make a hole in the indent with a cone tool and insert a marzipan stalk.

Spray or dust the green apples

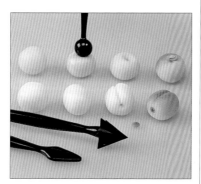

Stages of making the apples and peaches

with green colouring or dusting powder and add a blush of red on one side. Colour the natural marzipan with red colouring, creating a heavier patch to one side.

9 Use 10g (⅓oz/1 tablespoon) natural marzipan to make the peach. Roll into a ball, then roll and flatten slightly between the palms of your hands. Indent a line across the top with a blunt blade and make a hole at one end of this line. Colour very lightly with pale yellow, then add a blush of red across the top.

Stages of making the pears

10 For the two pears, colour 20g (¾oz) marzipan very pale green and then divide it into two equal portions.

Roll them into ball shapes. Hold your hands upright and place one ball shape between the base of your palms. Rock backwards and forwards to form the shape of the pear. Repeat with the other ball of marzipan. Indent a hole in the neck ends and insert a brown marzipan stalk in each.

Cut out two small stars from the brown marzipan. Press them on to the opposite ends and impress the centres with a star cone tool. Colour with a touch of green and a red blush on one side.

11 Arrange a ring of holly leaves around the top of the cake. Position them so that some point inwards and others outwards, and alternate the colours. Attach with a small amount of green royal icing.

Attaching the outer ring of holly

12 Arrange the marzipan fruits, in small clusters of two or three, on top of the holly leaves. Secure in place with a little royal icing.

Adding clusters of fruit

13 Add extra holly leaves at varying angles in between the clusters of fruit. Roll some small balls of red marzipan for berries and attach to the holly where the colour is needed.

Add a ribbon for further decoration

14 To finish you can place a wide organza ribbon around the side of the cake and attach at the front with royal icing. Secure with glass-headed pins until the icing is dry. Then add a large bow to cover the join.

Nine square sparkle

This simple design illustrates many of the traditional objects we associate with Christmas. The crisp white, blue and turquoise colour scheme adds a contemporary feel.

Cake and decoration

20cm (8in) square fruit cake
28cm (11in) square board
Apricot jam (jelly)
1kg (2lb/6 cups) marzipan
1kg (2lb/6½ cups) white sugarpaste (rolled fondant)
Clear alcohol
60g (2oz) flower paste
Blue and green paste food colourings
Mother-of-pearl, disco green and silver snow dusting powders (petal dust) [EA]
Small amount of royal icing
Silver dragées
Small amount of vegetable fat
Cornflour (cornstarch), for dusting
Painting solution [EA]
Edible glue
Silver ribbon for the edge of the board

Special equipment

Stencil card
Scriber or pin
Ruler
2.5cm (1in) round cutter
Designer wheel [PME]
Bobble tool [HP]
Nos. 1 and 17 piping tubes (tips) [PME]
Small and large plunger holly cutters
Small bell, cracker and tree cutters
Templates (see page 107)

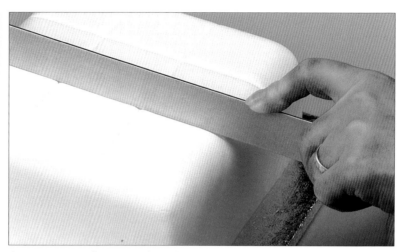

Creating nine equal squares with a ruler

1 Make a template for the top of the cake with stencil card by cutting an 18cm (7⅛in) square and dividing it into nine 6cm (2⅜in) squares. Cut a small V-shape in the edge on each division.

2 Place the cake on the cake board and brush with apricot jam (jelly). Roll out the marzipan and use to cover the cake. Roll out the sugarpaste (rolled fondant) to a 5mm (¼in) thickness. Brush the marzipan with clear alcohol and cover the cake with the sugarpaste. Trim the excess from the base and reserve.

3 While the sugarpaste is still soft, place the template on top of the cake. Mark the dividing points of the

Marking dividing points on the cake

template around the edges of the cake using a scriber or pin. Remove the template and use the edge of a ruler to impress lines across the sugarpaste, so that the marked points join. The final effect should be nine equal squares.

Indenting stitches with a designer wheel

4 Use a designer wheel to indent 'stitches' along the ruler-marked lines. Move slowly to prevent the wheel from slipping out of the indented groove and ruining the sugarpaste surface. Leave the coating to dry.

5 Colour two-thirds of the flower paste pale blue. Add green to half the blue paste to make turquoise. Colour the reserved sugarpaste turquoise.

Texturing the turquoise board covering

6 Roll out and cut strips of the turquoise sugarpaste and use to cover the cake board. Mitre the corners of the paste and remove the excess. Gently push the paste together at the joins and smooth it over with the tip of your finger to neaten.

7 Texture the sugarpaste by rolling a bobble tool backwards and forwards in short lengths over the surface. Gently ease the tool around the corners, keeping the pattern at ninety degrees to the edge of the cake board. Trim the board, brush the sugarpaste covering with mother-of-pearl dusting powder (petal dust).

Dusting the sugarpaste board covering

8 Put some royal icing in a bag fitted with a No.1 tube (tip) and use this to attach a silver dragée to each of the points where the grooves cross the top of the cake. Attach a dragée to the end of each of the lines with a bulb of royal icing.

Place a ruler against the side of the cake, resting on the board, and attach another line of silver dragées just

Aligning the row of dragées with a ruler

above it, so that they line up with the dragées on the top edge of the cake. Continue around the cake, adding two more rows of silver dragées. Continue around the cake, adding two more rows of silver dragées on each side, one at the base and one near the top edge, alternating with the previous rows.

9 Make the flower paste decorations for the top of the cake. Either trace the templates for all the designs or use small cutters for the circles, crackers, tree and bell. Coat the board with a very thin film of white vegetable fat and roll out the flower paste very thinly. Before cutting out

the shapes, turn the piece of paste over on to a surface lightly dusted with cornflour (cornstarch). Keep unused flower paste covered with cling film (plastic wrap) while you are working to prevent it from drying out.

10 Cut out the crown from blue flower paste using the template. Add a thin strip of turquoise paste at the base and two tiny triangles between the points. Paint a silver line along the edge of the points with dusting powder and painting solution.

11 For the bauble, cut out a circle with a diameter of about 2.5cm (1in) from the turquoise paste. Cut a curved band in blue with the same cutter and use this for the striped decoration. Add a bow at the top made from a narrow strip of the blue paste.

12 Cut out and vein a large holly leaf from turquoise flower paste with a plunger cutter. Use a knife to carefully cut out three small circles for holly berries from the blue flower

Stages in making the crown, bauble and holly leaf with flower paste

Stages in making the Christmas pudding, candles and bell

Stages in making the Christmas crackers, tree and parcel

paste and, using a No. 17 piping tube, add these to the leaf with a small bulb of icing .

13 To make the Christmas pudding, cut two 2.5cm (1in) diameter rounds, one in blue and one in white. Trim the white one by cutting a wavy line across it about one-third from the top.

Position the white paste shape over the blue disc. Add two small holly leaves in turquoise.

14 To make the candles, cut two 5mm (¼in) strips, 2.5cm (1in) long from the turquoise flower paste. Trim them diagonally so that the ends slant, as shown. For the flames, use two tear-drop shapes in white flower

paste. Add two blue holly leaves at the base of the candles.

15 Cut out a bell from the blue flower paste, using the template or a shaped cutter. Then, using the curved edge of the same cutter or following the same line of the template, cut a turquoise strip to decorate it. Use a No. 17 piping tube to cut a circle from the turquoise paste. Halve the circle and use this for the bell clapper. Paint the knob at the top of the bell with silver snow dusting powder mixed with painting solution or clear alcohol.

16 Cut out one Christmas cracker from the blue flower paste and another one from the turquoise, using

the template or a shaped cutter. Paint a band of silver across the indents with dusting powder and painting solution or clear alcohol.

17 Cut the Christmas tree out of turquoise paste, using the template or a shaped cutter. Paint the trunk with silver snow dusting powder and painting solution.

18 Using the template, cut out a parcel shape from turquoise paste. Use the back of a knife to mark lines dividing the parcel surfaces. Cut out thin strips of blue paste to add as the ribbon and bow.

19 Brush all of the cut-out pieces with mother-of-pearl dusting powder. Assemble the decorations on top of the cake, as shown, securing them in place with edible glue.

20 Sprinkle or brush disco green dusting powder over the top of all the decorations and along the turquoise board covering. Finally, add some silver ribbon to the edge of the board, to complement the silver dragées.

Helpful hints

• Try to use the edible glue sparingly, as it can squeeze out from under the decorations and make the edges appear messy.
• If royal icing is not available, soften some sugarpaste with cool, boiled water and use this for piping.

Three kings

This jewel-like cake shows the three kings, or wise men, following the star to Bethlehem.

Cake and decoration

2 x 15cm (6in) square fruit cakes

Apricot jam (jelly)

13cm (7in) and 20cm (8in) square cake boards

750g (1½lb/5 cups) marzipan

50g (1¾oz/⅓ cup) royal icing without glycerine

925g (2lb/6½ cups) sugarpaste

Ice blue, grape violet, black, holly green, autumn leaf, dark brown, mint green, melon, yellow, tangerine, claret paprika and baby blue (optional) paste food colourings

Blueberry, lavender/mauve and black magic airbrush colourings

380g (12½oz) modelling paste

Antique gold and silver [SK], mother-of-pearl [EA], claret wine lustre, African violet, jade and ice blue [S] dusting powders (petal dust)

Painting solution

Superwhite

White vegetable fat

Sugar glue

30g (1oz) pastillage (see page 97)

20g (¾oz) flower paste

0.75m (30in) 7mm (⅜in) navy ribbon

1m (1⅛yd) 1cm (½in) wide gold-edged burgundy ribbon for edge of board

Special equipment

Airbrush (optional)

Templates (see page 102)

Nos. 0 and 7 paintbrushes

Nos. 0, 1.5 and 2 piping tubes (tips)

Nos. 1 and 3 star cutters [FMM]

Frill cutter [OP]

Gold wires and 20 gauge wire

Classical Athens border beads [HH]

5cm (2in) Cel block ball [C]

Taffeta rolling pin [HP]

See pages 7 and 108 for the other cake side designs

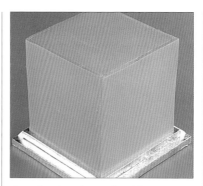

Covering the cake neatly with sugarpaste

1 Stick one cake on top of the other with apricot jam (jelly) and stick to the smaller cake board. Fill in the gap around the middle with a sausage of marzipan and trim. Brush the cake top with apricot jam.

Roll out the marzipan to 5mm (¼in) thick and use to cover the cake. Start with a piece for the top, then cover each side in turn, making the corners as neat and square as possible. Stick the cake in the centre of the larger board with royal icing. Leave to harden for a few days.

2 Colour 750g (1½lb/4¾ cups) sugarpaste (rolled fondant) with ice blue food colouring and roll out to 5mm (¼in) thick. Cover the cake with the sugarpaste, starting with the top, then the back, followed by the two sides and, finally, the front. Be careful when trimming the corners not to cut into the previous piece. Covering the cake in this order ensures there will be no joins on the front. Leave to harden for a couple of days.

3 If using an airbrush, shade the cake deep midnight blue. Start off with blueberry airbrush colouring, then use mauve/lavender and, finally, black magic to give an attractive cloudy effect. If you do not have an airbrush, it is possible to achieve a

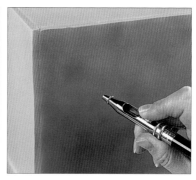

Colouring the cake with an airbrush

similar effect by stippling on food colourings mixed with a little water with a large stencil brush. Use baby blue, grape violet and black.

4 Using 175g (6oz/1⅛ cups) sugarpaste, fill in the area between the cake boards to achieve a bevelled edge. To do this, roll out the paste into a long sausage, wet the boards and squash the sausage in between. Press down with a smoother and trim away the excess with a sharp knife.

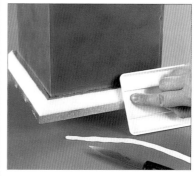

Smoothing the sugarpaste bevelled edge

5 Colour 110g (3½oz) modelling paste dark green with holly green and black food colourings, plus a little ice blue towards the end of mixing. Roll out and trim into a 23cm (9in) square. Cut into four long strips. Stick them to the cake board and over on to the bevelled edges. Mitre the corners and trim the excess at the lower edge.

6 Trace the design for the hill shapes on the sides. Knead the trimmings together and roll out quite thinly. Transfer the hill design to the sugarpaste four times. Cut around the shapes with a sharp knife and stick each one to the sides of the cake.

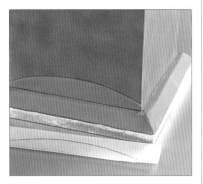

Sticking the hill shapes to the cake

7 Trace the designs for the three kings and their gifts. Mix the colours for the three kings and the stable scene. The quantities of modelling paste required for each colour are quite small, so for ease of handling, some of them have been rounded to 7g (¼oz) or 10g (⅓oz). The food colourings required are given in brackets below.
75g (2½oz) – gold (autumn leaf)
7g (¼oz) – brown (dark brown)
7g (¼oz) – green (mint and dark brown)
20g (¾oz) – ivory (a little autumn leaf)
10g (⅓oz) – purple (grape violet)
10g (⅓oz) – lime green (mint green and melon)
7g (¼oz) – yellow (yellow)
10g (⅓oz) – orange-yellow (yellow and tangerine)
100g (3½oz) – claret (claret)
7g (¼oz) – black (black)
10g (⅓oz) – flesh (paprika/dark brown)

8 For the Indian king, roll out a portion of the gold modelling paste and transfer the tracing of his boots to it. Cut around the pencil line with a sharp knife, flip over, brush a little water on the back and stick to the cake in the middle of one hill. Mark a line down the middle of his boots.

Continue building up the figure, using the tracing in the following order. Cut out the lower coat from claret paste (the triangle shape) and stick straight on to the cake above the boots, marking a line down the middle with a knife. Cut out the upper body from

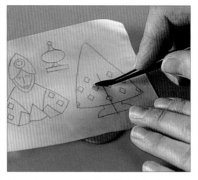

Transferring the Indian king's body

claret paste. Cut out the collar and cuffs from gold paste, stick to the upper body and then stick the whole upper body over the lower coat and on to the side of the cake.

Cut out the gift from gold paste and mark in lines. Roll out flesh-colour paste for his head. Cut out and stick in place. Roll out gold paste for his turban. Cut out and stick over the head. Mark lines with a veining tool.

Roll a small ball of flesh paste into a cone. Flatten, mark a line down the centre and stick on the coat to make his hands. Paint the collar, cuffs, diamonds, boots, turban and gift gold with gold dusting powder (petal dust) and painting solution. Paint in his features using black for the beard and dark brown and black for the eyes.

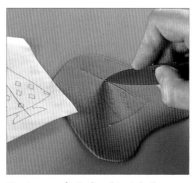

Cutting out the Indian king's body

9 For the Chinese king, build up the clothing in the same way: orange-yellow feet and legs, lime coat with an orange-yellow band at the bottom, lime upper body with an orange-yellow collar, flesh-colour head, claret hat (crown first, then the brim) and flattened cone for the hands. Use white for his gift and pipe handles with a No. 0 tube (tip). Roll a claret ball for the top and a sausage for the lid trim.

Paint circles of ice blue and superwhite with water on the king's coat, with radiating lines in orange-yellow. Paint the edge of the brim gold and lines of gold on the orange band. Paint the features in dark brown and black with a No. 0 brush.

Cutting out the Chinese king

10 For the Mongolian king, begin with gold shoes and black trousers. Use purple for the lower coat, with a lime green trim and a band of yellow at his hips. Make the upper body with purple paste, marking crossed lines with a knife to look like quilting. Add yellow arm bands and black cuffs. Make the head in flesh colour and the headdress in gold, marking in lines

Preparing the Mongolian king

with a knife. Roll black balls for his earmuffs. Cut out his gift in white, mark in the lid, pipe dots and cones for handles and a knob. Paint it silver. Paint red stripes on the band at his hips and red dots and stripes on his armbands. Paint gold on his feet, headdress, coat edging and gold dots on the quilting. Paint the features as before, but with a beard curling up.

11 Trace the stable, trees and star. Trace and cut out a white stable front, gold roof and dark brown tree trunks. Make green stars for the palm tree tops using the No. 1 star cutter. Stick to the back of the cake with the stable in the middle and a tree either side. Paint watery dark brown lines on the stable roof to look like straw. Paint the windows, door and tree trunks a darker shade of brown. Roll out the ivory paste and cut out a scalloped circle with the frill cutter. Stick above the stable with water. Roll out 15g (½oz) gold paste with a little white fat on the surface and the rolling pin. Dust with gold dusting powder.

Transfer the large star image to the paste and cut out with a sharp knife. Leave to dry overnight, then fix in place over the scalloped circle with a little royal icing. (Leaving the star overnight makes it easier to handle, as the gold smudges very easily while the paste is still soft.)

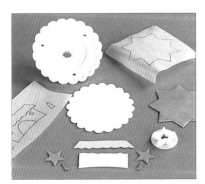

Cutting out the stable scene

12 Paint small dots and stars in the sky on each cake side with gold dusting powder and painting solution using a No. 0 brush. Stick navy blue ribbon to the top edge of the cake, mitring the corners to neaten the edges and hide the sugarpaste joins.

13 Colour 20g (⅔oz) flower paste autumn gold. Rub a little white fat into the surface of a nylon rolling pin and the work surface. Roll out the paste to 2mm (⅛in) thick. Dust the surface with a dry No. 7 brush and gold dusting powder, then flip the paste over and repeat. Cut out 16–20 stars with the No. 1 star cutter. Dip the ends of the gold wires into a little sugar glue and insert into the stars, being careful not to pierce the surface. Dip your fingers in the gold dust and rub into the surface of a length of 20 gauge wire.

Colour 30g (1oz) pastillage autumn leaf and dust each side with gold dusting powder. Cut out the large star using the star from stable scene. Dip the gold 20 gauge wire tip in sugar glue and insert into the star. Leave to dry on greaseproof or silicone paper.

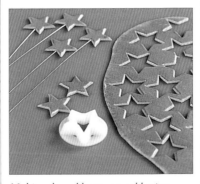

Making the gold stars on gold wires

14 Make the jewel borders for the top and bottom of the cake with 50g (1¾oz) autumn leaf modelling paste and the border mould. Dust the mould lightly with cornflour (cornstarch), roll a small piece of paste into a sausage and push into the mould. Trim off the excess and gently ease out of the mould. Stick to the top edge of the cake with royal icing and mitre the corners. Repeat to make continuous borders on the top and bottom of the cake, making all the joins as neat as possible. Paint in the ovals with alternating colours of African violet, combined jade and ice blue, mixed with mother-of-pearl, and claret wine lustre dusting powders mixed with dipping solution. Paint the background with gold dusting powder and painting solution.

Making the stars for the corners

15 Pipe the outlines of the corner stars four times with 40g (1¼oz/¼ cup) royal icing without glycerine on run-out film or waxed paper using a No. 2 tube. Leave to dry, then paint gold. Reserve one teaspoon of the icing and mix claret food colouring into the rest. Add water to make a run-out consistency. Flood in the star area. When dry, pipe a spiral over the surface with a No. 1.5 tube and remaining white icing. Leave the stars to dry again, then paint gold.

16 Cut the cel ball in half and stick one half to the cake surface, flat side down, using royal icing. Roll out 100g (3½oz) claret modelling paste into a 20cm (8in) square. Dust the paste with claret wine lustre dusting powder and a dry No. 7 brush, then texture the surface by rolling over with the taffeta rolling pin. Trim to an 18.5cm (7¼in) square, flip over and brush a line of water along each side. Roll the edges over and stick down.

Pipe a little royal icing on to the cel ball, lift the paste carefully and lay over the ball. Arrange the paste into pleasing folds and secure in place with dots of water where needed. Immediately insert the stars on wires and gold curls trimmed to appropriate lengths. Secure a length of gold-edged burgundy ribbon around the board.

Mistletoe ring

Associated with traditional Christmas celebrations, the pretty leaf and berry design provides a simple decoration for this brightly coloured cake.

Cake and decoration

18 x 23cm (7 x 9in) oval fruit cake
25 x 30cm (10 x 12in) oval cake board
Apricot jam (jelly)
1kg (2lb/6 cups) marzipan
Clear alcohol
1kg (2lb/6½ cups) poppy red sugarpaste (rolled fondant) [R]
180g (6oz) flower paste
Christmas green and brown paste food colourings [S]
Moss green [S] and lemon gold [EA] dusting powders (petal dust)
Cornflour (cornstarch)
125g (4oz/¾ cup) white sugarpaste
Edible glue
Painting solution [EA]
60g (2oz/⅓ cup) royal icing
Edible varnish [SK]
Gold ribbon for the edge of the board

Special equipment

1cm, 1.5cm and 2.5cm (½in, ¾in and 1in) straight leaf or petal cutters
Firm foam pad
Large ball tool [J]
Rose leaf veiner [OP]
Soft sponge
Small bell mould [PME]
Nos. 1.5 and 3 piping tubes (tips)
Template (see page 104)
Pin or scriber

1 Place the cake on the board. Brush with apricot jam (jelly). Roll out the marzipan and use to cover the cake.

2 Brush the surface with clear alcohol. Roll out the red sugarpaste (rolled fondant) and cover the cake. Trim the excess. Knead the trimmings, roll out again and cut two strips to cover the cake board. Lay the strips around the cake, overlapping at the joins, which should be at the two ends of the cake. Cut through both thicknesses of paste, remove the excess and pinch the edges together. Smooth over the join and trim away the excess paste from around the edge of the board. Leave to dry.

3 You will need about 20 small leaves, 70 medium and 12 large. Colour 125g (4oz) flower paste light green and roll out. Cut out the mistletoe leaves, using a plain leaf or petal cutter, and place on a firm foam pad. Stretch and thin the leaves with the large ball tool until they are double the original length and quite thin. Press each one on to a leaf veiner, then transfer to a piece of soft sponge, with the veins uppermost.

4 Press on the rounded end of the leaves with the large ball tool to cup and shape them, then twist slightly

Cutting, stretching and veining the leaves

before leaving them to dry. With practice, you will be able to cut and shape several leaves at a time.

Using the large ball tool on soft sponge

5 Mix some moss green dusting powder (petal dust) with cornflour (cornstarch) on a piece of kitchen paper (towel). Brush the leaves with the colour and place on a flat sieve. Vary the amount of cornflour to make several shades of green. Pass the sieve briefly over a jet of steam from a kettle (teakettle) to fix the colour. If you steam for too long, the leaves will dissolve and stick to the sieve.

Steaming the leaves to fix the colour

6 Mix together 60g (2oz/⅓ cup) white sugarpaste and the remaining white flower paste. To make a bell, roll a small piece into a ball, then into a cone, dust it with cornflour and place inside the bell mould. The correct amount of paste should just fill the

bottom of the bell, before the shape widens out. Push the large ball tool into the centre of the paste, twisting slightly at the same time to prevent it from sticking. With your fingers, press the paste which has been forced into the wider part of the mould against the sides, teasing it up to the rim.

Remove from the mould and dust with cornflour once more to stop the paste from sticking. Return the paste bell to the mould and leave for 10 minutes, until firm. Remove from the mould and leave to dry, standing on the rim. You will need six bells.

Stages of making the bells

7 Cut 60g (2oz/⅓ cup) sugarpaste into small pieces. Mash with a little edible glue to make a piping consistency. Pipe a line inside each bell from the centre to the rim, using a No. 3 tube (tip), and add a small ball of paste for a clapper. Leave to dry, then paint this and the rim of the bell with gold dusting powder mixed with painting solution or clear alcohol.

8 With the white paste left over from the bells, roll lots of small balls for the berries. Drop these into a small dish to stop them rolling all over the work surface. Leave to dry.

9 Cut out two triangular templates and place them in the centre of each long side of the cake. Colour the royal icing green and place in a piping bag with a No.1.5 tube. Pipe a random wavy line from the top of the triangles all around the base of the cake, then remove the templates.

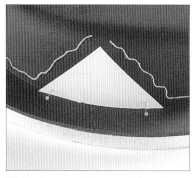

Piping the green line around the cake

10 Arrange pairs of leaves all the way along this line at differing angles, with some resting on the board and some sticking up the side of the cake. Use the royal icing to attach the leaves and to pipe a bud over the centre joint of each pair. Leave plenty of space around the area where the bells will be; more leaves can be added when the bells are in place.

11 Attach clusters of two, three or four berries along the line between the leaves. When the icing is dry, apply four tiny dots to the top of each berry by dipping a pin or scriber into brown paste colouring and touching this on the surface.

Attaching the leaves and piping the buds

12 Arrange three bells at each side of the cake, as shown, attaching them with some sugarpaste softened to a piping consistency. As they are quite heavy, you will need to support them with foam until they are dry. If you have difficulty making them stay in position, attach only one at a time, allowing it to dry completely before adding the next one.

Attaching and supporting the bells

13 Add a few more leaves around and above the bells, continuing just on to the top of the cake. Paint some of the smallest leaves gold and, when dry, mix them in with the leaves around the bells and at random around the base of the cake.

Adding extra leaves including gold ones

14 Brush all the leaves, buds and berries with edible varnish and leave to dry. Attach a gold ribbon around the edge of the cake board.

Helpful hints

• If you do not have a flat sieve, use a splatter guard. The large flat surface allows you to lay out and steam a lot of leaves at the same time.
• To avoid the paste sticking in the mould, keep removing it and dust with cornflour (cornstarch). You can also use equal parts cornflour and icing (confectioners') sugar for a lighter dusting mixture.
• Mixing sugarpaste with edible glue makes a stronger solution for attaching heavy ornaments, such as the bells.

Eastern star

The star in the East and the three wise men is a popular Christmas story. Here, it is translated into a modern interpretation and colour scheme, decorated with simple cut outs.

Cake and decoration

20cm (8in) square fruit cake
Apricot jam (jelly)
1kg (2lb/6 cups) marzipan
28cm (11in) square cake board
Clear alcohol
1kg (2lb/6½ cups) violet sugarpaste (rolled fondant)
125g (4oz/¾ cup) white sugarpaste
125g (4oz) white flower paste
Vegetable fat
Cornflour (cornstarch), for dusting
Claret, violet or purple and navy paste food colourings [S]
Lemon gold dusting powder (petal dust) [EA]
Painting solution [EA]
60g (2oz/⅓ cup) royal icing
Navy velvet ribbon for the edge of the board

Special equipment

3cm, 1.5cm and 1cm (1¼in, ¾in and ½in) triangular cutters [CCS]
Templates (see page 105)
Run-out film
Nos. 1.5 and 3 piping tubes (tips)
Glue stick

1 Brush the cake with apricot jam (jelly). Roll out the marzipan and use to cover the top and sides. Place the cake on the board and brush with clear alcohol. Roll out the violet sugarpaste (rolled fondant) and use to cover the cake. Trim the excess.

2 Roll out the trimmings and cut four strips to cover the board. Overlap them at the corners and cut through both thicknesses from the corner of the cake to the corner of the board. Pinch the edges together, smooth over the join with your finger and finish off with a smoother. Leave to dry.

3 Mix together 30g (1oz/⅜ cup) white sugarpaste and 30g (1oz) flower paste and set to one side. Mix the remaining sugarpaste and flower paste and colour to a medium claret, adding a tiny amount of purple. Reserve one-third of the medium claret paste. Add more purple food colouring to the remainder. Reserve half the purple paste. Add navy to the remainder.

4 Roll out the purple paste on a lightly greased board. Turn it on to a surface dusted with cornflour (cornstarch) and cut out 40 purple triangles with the largest cutter. Cut out 40 triangles from the navy paste with the medium cutter. Cut out 40 triangles from the

Mixing claret, purple and navy paste

claret paste with the smallest cutter and 40 white ones. When dry, paint the white shapes with gold dusting powder and painting solution.

Cutting out and painting the triangles

5 Trace the patterns for the stars on to thin card and cut out to use as templates. Roll out each colour of paste thinly and place on a small board covered with thick run-out film. Smooth down, pressing it on to the film, then cut out each star with a sharp knife using the templates; the largest in purple, medium in navy and smallest in white. If you use a separate board for each one, it will be easier to keep rotating the surface so that you can cut from the centre outwards, resulting in a neater appearance. Leave to dry. Remove by sliding a thin palette knife (metal spatula) underneath. Paint the white star gold.

Cutting out a large star with a template

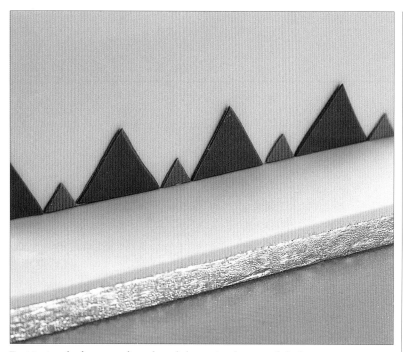

Positioning the first row of purple and claret triangles around the base

6 Soften the remaining violet sugarpaste (used for the coating) with water to a piping consistency and place in a No. 3 tube. Use for attaching the cut-outs. To decorate the first side of the cake, start by attaching a purple triangle in the centre of the bottom edge and one at each corner, then arrange two more, equally spaced in between.

Alternate these with tiny claret coloured pieces as shown. Only work on one side at a time while the piped sugarpaste remains wet, allowing you to move them along, if necessary, so that they fit correctly.

7 Add the matching board pieces, lining them up with the sides.

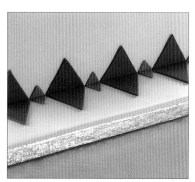

Lining up the board pieces

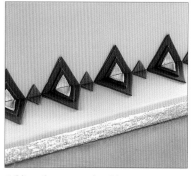

Adding the navy and gold pieces

8 Attach the navy triangles, then the gold triangles, over the large purple triangles on the cake and the board. Using white royal icing in a No.1.5 tube, pipe a continuous line around the pattern on the board. When this is dry, paint it gold.

Piping around the pattern on the board

Piping radiating lines from the star

9 To decorate the top of the cake, assemble the three layers of the star and attach towards the right-hand side. Pipe radiating lines between the points of the star, as shown, and paint them gold when they are dry.

10 Finish off the edge of the cake board with navy velvet ribbon. The easiest way to attach this is with a solid glue stick.

Helpful hints

• When mixing violet for a covering, start with pale blue paste and add violet or purple to achieve the colour required. Violet shades fade very quickly but, if the base colour is pale blue, it will fade to this.

• When you are not working on the cake, keep it in a box with a close-fitting lid, or in a dark cupboard, to prevent fading.

• To make sure that several colours blend together, always start with the same base colour.

• Each time you use a cutter, wipe the edge with a dry cloth to ensure a clean cut every time. Neat edges on the cut-out pieces will fit together better.

• If you do not have the appropriate cutters, cut the triangles from strips 3cm, 1.5cm and 1cm (1⅛in, ¾in and ½in) wide.

• When painting a fine piped line, load the brush liberally with the solution and wipe along the top of the line with the side of the bristles.

Star of Bethlehem

Here is a contemporary depiction of the story of Christmas nativity, with strong, rich colours combining to create a cake of distinction.

Cake and decoration

20cm (8in) round fruit cake

Apricot jam (jelly)

1kg (2lb/6 cups) marzipan

28cm (11in) round cake board

750g (1½lb/4½ cups) white sugarpaste (rolled fondant)

Yellow, brown, orange, blue, purple, green and black paste food colourings

Clear alcohol

Brown, orange, yellow, blue, white and lemon gold [EA] dusting powders (petal dust)

Cornflour (cornstarch)

250g (8oz/1½ cups) blackcurrant sugarpaste [R]

60g (2oz) pastillage (see page 97)

Icing (confectioners') sugar, for dusting

Painting solution [EA]

Gold ribbon for the edge of the board

Special equipment

5mm (¼in) spacers [SSS]

Large star cutter [W]

Petal veining tool [HP]

Run-out film

2.5cm (1in) star cutter [K]

Template (see page 106)

Airbrush (optional)

Nos. 0, 1 and 3 sable paint brushes

Sugarpaste gun with grass and trefoil inserts

1 Brush the cake with apricot jam (jelly). Roll out the marzipan and cover the cake. Place on the board and leave it to dry for at least 24 hours.

2 Colour the white sugarpaste (rolled fondant) to pale sand, using yellow, brown and orange. Brush the cake with clear alcohol, leaving a 7.5cm (3in) area in the centre. Roll out the sugarpaste to 5mm (¼in) thick and cover the cake. Cut through the paste in the centre with the large star cutter.

Lifting the cut-out sugarpaste star

Lift a point of the star with the tip of a knife, then pull upwards and remove the shape. Leave the coating to dry.

3 Airbrush around the base of the cake with a mixture of brown, orange and yellow, graduating to a lighter shade halfway up the sides. Spray around the edges of the star.

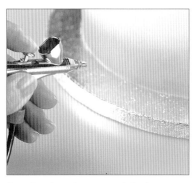

Spraying the colour around the base

Alternatively, mix the same colours of dusting powder (petal dust) and add an equal quantity of cornflour (cornstarch). Brush on the cake, then rub the powder into the surface with a small piece of kitchen paper (towel), using a circular movement.

4 Mix blue food colouring into the blackcurrant sugarpaste to make a rich purple colour. Roll out and cut 5cm (2in) wide strips to cover the board. Moisten the board with water

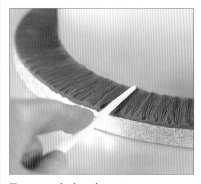

Texturing the board covering

and place the strips around the cake, overlapping at the joins. Cut through both thicknesses, press the two ends together and smooth with your finger. Pattern the paste by rolling a petal veining tool backwards and forwards, in short lengths, all around the cake, keeping it at a right angle to the edge of the board. Trim the excess paste from the edge.

5 Place a piece of run-out film on a small, flat board, and secure at the corners. Roll out the pastillage very thinly on a surface dusted with icing (confectioners') sugar. Place the pastillage over the board, and cut out five small stars and one large star. Remove the excess paste and leave the stars on the board until dry. Try slotting the large one into the hole in

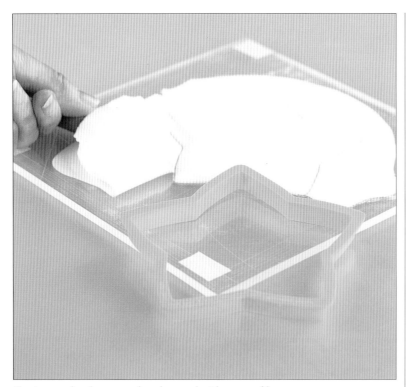

Cutting out the plaque on a board covered with run-out film

8 Next, paint in the windows and doors, and the nativity figures, in black. To paint in the trees, use dark green, and, with an almost dry paintbrush, dab on the paint to create a bushy effect. Finish them off with a few dabs of black.

Outline all the buildings with a black line. Use only the tip of the paintbrush, in an upright position, to paint very fine lines.

9 Paint the domes of the buildings and the stars with gold dusting powder mixed with painting solution or clear alcohol. The alcohol will run very slightly into the background colour and create a blue halo around each star.

Using a scalpel, scratch the surface of the plaque to reveal white highlights on some of the windows and roofs of the buildings.

the top of the cake to make sure that it fits. If it is a tight fit, shave away a little of the sugarpaste from inside the star cut out on the cake.

6 Trace the pattern of the Christmas scene and transfer to the plaque.

Airbrush the sky with dark blue, getting lighter towards the horizon, or use blue dusting powder mixed with a little cornflour. Brush on, then carefully rub into the surface with a small piece of kitchen paper (towel).

Place the plaque upside down in a wire sieve and pass briefly through the jet of steam from a kettle to fix the colour. Leave to dry.

7 Mix each colour for painting the plaque. Use clear alcohol and white dusting powder to lighten where required. The colours will dry very quickly, so add more alcohol as necessary. Use the No. 3 brush for painting the larger areas, the No. 1 brush for filling in smaller ones and the No. 0 brush for outlining and details.

First, paint in the background colours of the buildings, using shades of brown in the foreground and blues and purples in the background. Fill in the outline of the stable with yellow, brightening to white in the centre. Paint the area where the trees are, across the centre, in light green.

Painting the windows, doors and figures

10 Paint the inside edge of the cut-out star on top of the cake in gold, and extend the painting inwards slightly on to the marzipan below. If your plaque has shrunk at all, only the

Steaming the plaque to fix the colour

Painting in the background colours

Finished plaque

Painting the inside edge of the cut-out on top of the cake

Painting the rope around the base

13 Paint the tassels and the rope with gold dusting powder mixed with painting solution. Paint the five small stars and fix over the ends of the tassels. Attach a gold ribbon to the edge of the board.

Helpful hints

gold colour will show around the painted plaque. Place the plaque in position. Someone may wish to keep the plaque, so do not stick it down – this also makes it easy to remove before the cake is cut.

11 To make the tassels, colour a small amount of sugarpaste yellow and soften with cool, boiled water. Shape into a roll and place in a sugarpaste gun.

There are usually three sizes of grass inserts. Use the largest one for the tassels. Alternatively, you can use a garlic press, but the strands will be thicker. Press out the strands of paste

long enough to hang down the side of the cake. Drape over the side in line with the indents of the star on top, so that the tips of the tassel rest about 1cm (½in) above the board. Break the paste away from the gun, press the tops of the strands together and attach the tassel 1cm (½in) away from the edge of the star.

12 Insert the largest trefoil shape into the sugarpaste gun and press out two long lengths. Twist the lengths of paste to make a rope effect and place around the base of the cake, trimming each end on a slant so that they fit together without showing the join.

• Use 5mm (¼in) spacers to roll out the sugarpaste (rolled fondant). This ensures that it will be an even thickness throughout.
• Do not use dusting powders (petal dust) directly on the cake surface without mixing with cornflour (cornstarch). Otherwise, the surface will become blotchy.
• When you require a deep colour of sugarpaste, it helps to begin with paste that you have purchased ready-coloured. This prevents the paste becoming extremely soft and difficult to handle.
• Cutting out a plaque on a prepared board prevents unnecessary transferring, which may distort the shape.
• Pastillage dries to a very hard and brittle texture, so keep the plaque on a solid surface and do not apply too much pressure.
• Rub some vegetable fat on to your hands before softening the paste for the rope; this prevents it from sticking.
• Ensure that the barrel of the sugarpaste gun is full before making the ropes; otherwise, there may not be enough paste to make sufficiently long ropes.

Making and positioning the tassels

Making the rope for the base of the cake

Yuletide slices

These small, decorated slices of fruit
cake make ideal gifts. Try making two or three
designs and arranging them in an attractive gift box.

Stars

Cake and decoration

Fruit cake

Apricot jam (jelly)

Marzipan

Clear alcohol

Pale blue sugarpaste (rolled fondant)
(As a guide, 250g (8oz) will cover
three slices)

White flower paste

Blue and lemon gold dusting
powders (petal dust) [EA]

Cornflour (cornstarch)

Painting solution [EA]

Small amount of royal icing

Special equipment

5mm (¼in) spacers

Small star cutter [PME]

Large star cutter [CK]

Paintbrush

1 Bake the fruit cake in a square
tin (pan). Cut it into 2.5cm (1in) slabs.
Lay the cake down on its side and,
if necessary, trim the top and sides
straight. Brush the slabs with apricot
jam (jelly). Roll out the marzipan
and use to cover the top and ends.
Brush with clear alcohol. Roll out the
sugarpaste (rolled fondant) between
the spacers and use to cover again.
Leave for 24 hours to dry, then cut into
3cm (1½in) slices, ready for decoration.

2 Mix together a little blue dusting
powder (petal dust) and cornflour
(cornstarch) to make a darker shade
of blue than the sugarpaste covering.
Brush on to the top of the slice.

3 Roll out the flower paste and cut
out one large and three small stars.
Paint the edges of the stars with gold
dusting powder mixed with painting
solution. Attach them to the top of
the cake slice with royal icing.

Stages of cutting and covering the slice

Cutting the stars ready for painting

Trees

Cake and decoration

White sugarpaste (rolled fondant)

White flower paste

Slices of fruit cake covered in pale blue sugarpaste (for method see *Stars*, page 71)

Edible glue

Lemon gold dusting powder (petal dust) [EA]

Painting solution [EA]

Small amount of royal icing

Special equipment

Ribbed rolling pin [PME]

Small tree cutter [PME]

Paintbrush

1 Roll out a piece of white sugarpaste (rolled fondant) and texture with a ribbed rolling pin. Cut out a right-angled triangle 8cm (3in) high and 3cm (1¼in) at the base. The longest edge should align with the lines of the ribbing. Place the triangle on top of the slice, attaching with a little edible glue.

Cutting out and attaching the triangle

2 Cut out two trees from the flower paste and leave to dry. Paint their edges with gold dusting powder (petal dust) mixed with painting solution. Attach them to the slice, as shown, with large bulbs of royal icing to lift them high enough to overlap the edge of the triangle.

Adding the trees to the slice

Ribbon and bells

Cake and decoration

White flower paste

Buttercup and old gold liquid food colourings [S]

Lemon gold dusting powder (petal dust) [EA]

Painting solution [EA]

Red flower paste

Slices of fruit cake covered in white sugarpaste (rolled fondant) (for method, see *Stars*, page 71)

Edible glue

Small amount of royal icing

Edible varnish [SK]

Special equipment

Small bell cutter [PME]

Medium paintbrush

1 Colour a small amount of white flower paste with equal quantities of buttercup and old gold liquid food colouring. Roll out thinly and cut out three bells. Place them on a flat surface and leave to dry.

2 When the bells are dry, paint the edges with gold dusting powder (petal dust) mixed with painting solution, using a medium-size paintbrush. Leave to dry.

3 Roll out the red flower paste thinly and cut a narrow strip about 13cm (5in) long. Drape the ribbon along the length of the cake slice, attaching it with edible glue.

4 Add the three bells and pipe on the clappers with white royal icing. When dry, paint them with gold dusting powder (petal dust) mixed with painting solution. Brush the ribbon with edible varnish to finish.

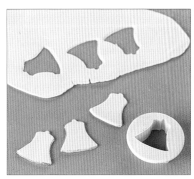

Cutting out the flower paste bells

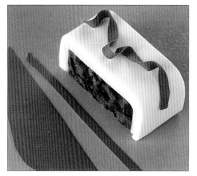

Cutting out and attaching the ribbon

Taffeta and holly

Cake and decoration

Red sugarpaste (rolled fondant)

Slices of fruit cake covered in white sugarpaste (for method, see *Stars*, page 71)

Red copper satin [EA] and dark green dusting powders (petal dust)

Edible glue

Green flower paste

Dark green liquid food colouring (optional)

Small amount of royal icing

Gold dragées

Special equipment

Taffeta rolling pin [HP]

Paintbrush

Medium plunger holly cutter [PME]

Airbrush (optional)

1 Roll out the red sugarpaste (rolled fondant) and texture it using the taffeta rolling pin. Cut a neat strip 1.5cm (⅝in) wide and brush with the red copper satin dusting powder (petal dust).

2 Place the sugarpaste strip along one side of the slice of cake, extending the two ends down to the base, and attach it with edible glue. Trim the edges level with the base using a sharp knife.

3 Roll out the green flower paste and cut out three holly leaves. Twist them slightly and then leave to dry.

4 Brush the edges of the holly leaves with dark green dusting powder and steam to seal the colour. Alternatively, airbrush the edges of the leaves with dark green food colouring.

5 Attach the leaves to the top of the slice with royal icing and add gold dragées for the berries.

Cutting out taffeta strip and dusting

Taffeta strip in place with leaf stages at side

Fruits

Cake and decoration

Brown sugarpaste (rolled fondant)

Gold, green and red dusting powders (petal dust)

Slices of fruit cake covered in cream-coloured sugarpaste (for method, see *Stars*, page 71)

Pink, green and orange marzipan

Small amount of green flower paste

Special equipment

Fine rib rolling pin [HP]

Paintbrush

Large ball tool [J]

Fluted cone tool [J]

Wire sieve

Small plunger holly cutter [PME]

Miniature star cutter [PME]

1 Roll out the brown sugarpaste (rolled fondant) thinly and texture with the rib rolling pin. Cut out a rectangle 3.5 x 1cm (1⅜ x ½in), brush with gold dusting powder (petal dust) and place across one end of the cake slice.

2 Roll some pink marzipan into a small ball and indent the top with a large ball tool. Cut the ball in half and add a stalk at the top. Roll the green marzipan into a pear shape and cut

in half. Cut out a small brown star and add half of it to the base. Then brush the surface of the apple and pear with green and red dusting powders.

3 Roll a small ball of orange marzipan and texture by rolling on to the surface of a wire sieve. Cut in half, then indent the top with the fluted cone. Place the three fruits on top of the slice and add two small holly leaves cut out of flower paste.

Making the brown rectangle

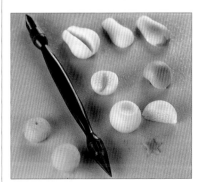

Stages of making the marzipan fruits

Christmas rose

Cake and decoration

White and green flower paste

Green dusting powder (petal dust)

Yellow paste colouring

Yellow Sugartex [S]

Edible glue

Edible varnish [SK]

Slices of fruit cake covered in turquoise sugarpaste (rolled fondant) (for method, see *Stars*, page 71)

Special equipment

Small petunia cutter [TKT]

Firm foam pad

Soft foam pad

Large ball tool [J]

No. 16 piping tube (tip) [PME]

Small rose leaf [SC]

Rose leaf veiner

1 Roll out the white flower paste and cut out the flower with the small petunia cutter. Thin the edges on a firm foam pad. Place the flower on a soft foam pad and press in the centre of the flower and the centre of the petals with the ball tool to make the cupped shape. Leave to dry.

2 When dry, dust in the middle of the flower with green dusting powder (petal dust) and paint yellow stamens radiating from the centre.

3 Cut out a tiny circle of white paste using a No. 16 piping tube (tip). Brush with edible glue, sprinkle with yellow Sugartex and place in the middle of the flower.

4 Cut two rose leaves from the green flower paste. Press on to a veiner, twist slightly and leave to dry. Dust darker green around the edges and steam, before painting with edible varnish. Attach the leaves and flower to the top of the slice as shown.

Stages of making the Christmas rose

Stages of making and attaching the leaves

Partridge in a pear tree

According to the popular Christmas song, 'my true love gave to me, a partridge in a pear tree'. It is not exactly an attractive bird, so a little artistic licence has been used to brighten up this cake.

Cake and decoration

20cm (8in) square fruit cake
Apricot jam (jelly)
1kg (2lb/6 cups) marzipan
25 x 35cm (10 x 14in) cake board
250g (8oz) modelling paste
Mint green, gooseberry, dark brown, Christmas red, tangerine, holly green, spruce green, grape violet, autumn leaf, ice blue, navy, black and egg yellow paste food colourings
1kg 25g (2¼lb/6⅔ cups) sugarpaste (rolled fondant)
Rose dusting powder (petal dust) [EA]
Superwhite
Dipping solution
Small amount of royal icing
Gold ribbon for the edge of the board

Special equipment

Templates (see page 107)
Smoother
Veining tool
Nos. 0 and 42 piping tubes (tips)
355 daisy cutter [FCC]
Sugarcraft gun
Small blossom cutter [PME]
No. 0 paintbrush
Jasmine leaf cutter

1 Shape the cake. Measure in from one side and cut off a 5 x 20cm (2 x 8in) rectangle. Spread a little apricot jam (jelly) down one short side of the large cake. Stick the rectangle to it. Trim off the piece that juts out, so it is flush with the side of the large cake. Make a template from card and use it to cut the curve of the top from the rest of the cake. Stick it in place with apricot jam. Brush the cake top with apricot jam. Roll out the marzipan and use to cover the top sides, then place on the cake board and leave to harden overnight.

Cutting and sticking to shape the cake

2 Make a card template for the window. Colour 50g (1¾oz) modelling paste with mint green, gooseberry and dark brown food colourings to make a pale green. Colour 350g (12oz/2¼ cups) sugarpaste (rolled fondant) a reddish orange colour with

Smoothing over the card template

Christmas red, tangerine and a little dark brown. Roll out into a rectangle large enough to cover the cake. Moisten the top of the cake, lay over the paste and smooth the top. Trim off the excess paste at the edges. Immediately position the card template over the top and press down with the smoother so the template presses into the paste and leaves an impression behind. Carefully remove the template. Roll out the pale green modelling paste to the same thickness as the card template. Lay the template on the top and cut around it.

Cutting out the modelling paste window

Paint a line of water on top of the cake just inside the indented line. Lift and lower the paste on to the cake and press down with a smoother so that it fits inside the red border neatly. Try to make sure there are no air bubbles trapped underneath.

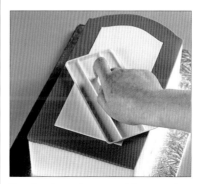

Pressing down the paste with a smoother

3 Colour 425g (14oz/2¾ cups) sugarpaste pale green. Roll out into a long strip, trim one long edge and stick to the side of the cake, trimmed edge down. Make a join at a corner. Smooth and trim the top edge against the top of the cake. Leave to dry.

Transferring the partridge and pear tree

Positioning the leaves around the pot

4 Trace the pear tree and bird from the template and transfer to the top of the cake. Position it centrally so that the bushy part of the tree overlaps by the same amount each side.

5 Colour 35g (1¼oz) modelling paste light green with gooseberry and mint green, and 85g (3oz) dark green with a mix of gooseberry, holly green and spruce green. Take 10g (⅓oz) of each colour and reserve the remainder. Roll out both the greens into long rectangles. Cut the dark green into thin strips about 1cm (⅜in) wide, flip over, moisten the back and lay over the light green paste. Roll both colours together and use immediately to cut out the leaves for the top of the cake. Lay the tracing over the paste, pencil side down, lining up the leaf so

that the centre line is over the join of the colours and rub over one leaf at a time with the veining tool. You may need to curve the paste to get the centre of the leaf tracing to match up. Moisten the corresponding area of the cake with water and stick in place. Soften the edges with your fingers, then mark in veins with a sharp knife.

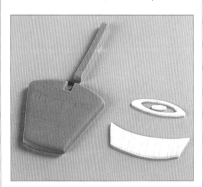

Pieces for the pot and tree trunk

6 Colour 20g (⅔oz) modelling paste with grape violet, then roll out to 3mm (⅛in) thick. Use the tracing to cut the plant pot and tree trunk. Stick to the cake and round off the edges by smoothing over with your fingers. Roll out 7g (¼oz) white modelling paste quite thinly. Using the tracing, cut out the circles for the top and the rim of the pot. Stick to the corresponding areas on the cake.

Texturing the surface of the pear tree

7 Roll out 60g (2oz) dark green modelling paste to 3mm (⅛in) thick. Using the tracing, cut out the oval for the tree. Stick to the cake, round off the edges with your fingers and texture the surface by pushing in the end of a No. 42 piping tube (tip).

8 Roll a tiny ball of purple modelling paste for the leg and another for the foot into a sausage with a bulge at each end to make the foot. Stick the foot and leg to the cake at the top of the tree. Roll out 10g (⅓oz) of white paste to 3mm (⅛in) thick. Using the tracing, cut out the partridge. Stick the bird just above the leg and soften the edges with your fingers. Re-roll the paste and cut out a separate wing. Stick the wing in position, so that the tip is just protruding beyond its back.

Cutting out the leaves for the pot

Cutting out the partridge

9 Colour 35g (1¼oz) modelling paste with autumn leaf and roll out seven balls about 1cm (½in) across using 10g (⅓oz) paste. Put a little gold dusting powder in the palm of your hand and roll a ball in the gold. Use a paintbrush handle to indent about two-thirds up the ball by rolling backwards and forwards. Make a hole with the veining tool at the top and bottom. Repeat for the other six. Stick to the tree with water.

Shaping the pears

10 Roll out a little dark green paste quite thinly and cut out a few daisy shapes with the daisy cutter. Cut out separate petals with a point at each end to make leaves. You will need a total of 14 leaves. Stick the leaves to the tops of the pears. Put a small sausage of dark green paste in a sugarcraft gun fitted with a fine mesh. Extrude small bunches to make foliage. Trim off at the gun with a knife and stick straight on to the tree.

11 Colour 10g (⅓oz) modelling paste blue using a mixture of ice blue and navy food colourings. Roll out the paste quite thinly. Cut out some little

Cutting out leaves and flowers

flowers using the small blossom cutter, and stick them on to the tree. Pipe small dots in the centres of the flowers, little dots on the tree and two claws for the partridge.

12 Paint black stripes on the rim of the pot and little stars made up of five lines on the top of the background. Paint the partridge using a little water and superwhite for each colour. Use navy and ice blue colourings for the beak and Christmas red for the neck, with a slight hint of grape violet in front. Paint the body with pale egg yellow food colouring and add light, feathery pairs of lines in holly green

over the top. Paint the bird's back with grape violet colouring. Paint black spots on the wing and a black streak across the head, with a circle and a dot for the eye. Paint a few black lines on the tail and legs.

Helpful hint

The gold dusting powder should stick quite easily to soft paste. If it does not, rub a little white vegetable fat into the palms of your hands when forming the balls, clean your hands and then roll the balls in the powder. This will help the dust adhere to the paste.

13 Roll out the remaining autumn leaf colour modelling paste into a rectangle about 30cm (12in) long and 3mm (⅛in) thick. Using a ruler, mark the paste rectangle into four strips about 8mm (⅜in) wide and cut them out against the edge of the ruler. Moisten the edges of the cake with water and lay the strips of paste over them so that they line up exactly with the edge of the cake. To mitre the corners, overlap the paste strips, then, using a sharp knife, cut through both layers of paste, in one go, at an angle of 45 degrees. Remove the pieces that were cut and smooth over the joins with your finger.

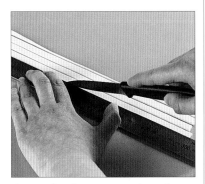

Cutting the edging strips with a ruler

14 Roll out 250g (8oz) white modelling paste into a rectangle about 35cm (14in) long. Cut into four thin strips, moisten the cake board and lay the strips of paste on the board. Mitre the corners by overlapping the paste, then, using a sharp knife, cut through both layers of paste, in one go, at an angle of 45 degrees. Remove the pieces that were cut, then smooth the join with your fingers.

Mitring the corners of the white paste

Making the dark and light green leaves for the base of the cake

15 Press a knife into the paste to create radiating lines. Leave to dry, then paint in alternate stripes with gold dusting powder and painting solution. Paint the frame on the top.

Making radiating lines

16 Make the leaves for the base of the cake in the same way as those on top of it using the remaining light and dark green paste (see step 5). Cut out leaves using the jasmine leaf cutter. Mark pairs of lines to look like veins using the blade of a knife. Shape the leaves with your hands to give them a realistic look and stick them around the base of the cake with a small amount of royal icing.

17 Paint in black stars, consisting of five little lines, on the sides of the cake using a No. 0 brush. Use a glue stick to glue a length of gold ribbon to the edge of the cake board.

Festive drapes

Elegant drapes are combined with holly and fruits to create this sophisticated Christmas cake. The design is easily adapted to any size of round cake by adding extra swags.

Cake and decoration

18cm (7in) round fruit cake
Apricot jam (jelly)
1kg (2lb/6 cups) marzipan
25cm (10in) round cake board
Clear alcohol
1kg (2lb/6½ cups) celebration sugarpaste (rolled fondant) [R]
250g (8oz/1⅔ cups) poppy red sugarpaste [R]
125g (4oz) white flower paste
Edible glue
Red copper satin, silver snow and lemon gold dusting powders (petal dust) [EA]
Painting solution [EA]
Matching ribbon for the edge of the board

Special equipment

Textured rolling pin [OP]
Scriber
7.5cm (3in) round cutter
Glass-headed pins
5 plastic cake dowels
Thin foam
Large and medium plunger holly cutters [PME]

1 Brush the cake with apricot jam (jelly). Roll out the marzipan and use to cover the top and side of the cake. Trim the excess with a sharp knife and reserve the remaining marzipan for making the fruits.

Place the cake on the board and brush with clear alcohol. Roll out the celebration-coloured sugarpaste (rolled fondant) and use to cover the cake. Trim away the excess at the base.

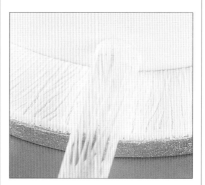

Rolling over the joins for continuity

2 Brush the board with water. Roll out the remaining sugarpaste to 2.5mm (⅛in) thick, then roll with the textured rolling pin. Cut out two 30 x 5cm (12 x 2in) strips. Use them to cover the board, taking care not to stretch the paste. Overlap at the joins and cut through both thicknesses, removing the excess paste. Using the end of the textured rolling pin, roll over the joins. Leave to dry for 24 hours.

The marzipan fruit and holly leaves

3 Prepare a paper template the same circumference and depth as the cake. Fold this in two and mark the halfway point down the fold. Open up and place a ruler between the top right-hand edge of the template and the halfway mark and draw a line. Open and continue the line down to the opposite left-hand corner, creating a diagonal line for the full length of the template. Cut along this line.

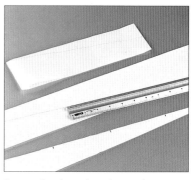

Stages of making the side template

4 Starting at the top, divide the sloped edge at 11cm (4½in) intervals. Place the template around the cake and secure with glass-headed pins. Mark the cake at each division of the template with a scriber, starting on the top edge and spiralling around it. Fold an 18cm (7in) disc of greaseproof (wax baking) paper into four, place on top of the cake and mark the centre. Remove the templates.

Marking the top of the cake

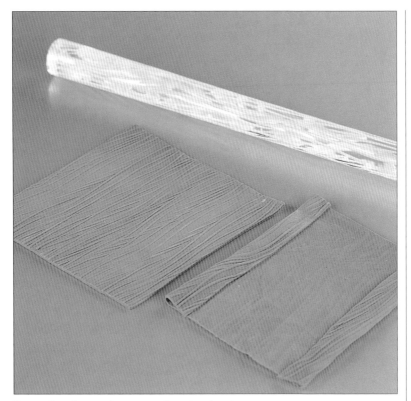

Stages of cutting out the swags and turning the edges

Attaching the first swag from the top

5 For the swags and bows, mix together 250g (8oz/1⅔ cups) red sugarpaste and the flower paste.

Make a square card template for the swag pattern 10 x 10cm (4 x 4in). Roll out the paste thinly and texture with the special rolling pin. Cut a square using the template. Turn the paste over, brush a small amount of edible glue along two opposite edges and turn them in about 5mm (¼in). Make sure the textured grain runs lengthways along the swag. Do not press the folded edges down as the rounded edge creates a soft fabric effect. Turn over and brush with red copper satin dusting powder (petal dust). Drag the brush across the texturing so that the dusting powder enhances the pattern.

6 Place two plastic dowels on a piece of thin foam, about 2.5cm (1in) apart. Drape the piece of paste over the top, then place three more dowels on top, positioning them so that they alternate with the two dowels under the paste. Press down gently to shape into folds.

7 Slide the dowels out and gather the paste together at the two ends, using the created folds. Make sure that the top and bottom folded edges are

Forming the folds with plastic dowels

Gathering and trimming the swags

facing backwards, then pinch firmly to stick all the folds together and press down. This is to allow space for the bow covering between the swags. If you need to use glue, do so sparingly.

8 Hold the swag at the two ends and stretch it slightly, then trim the ends to neaten. Moisten the back with edible glue and attach it to the cake between the scribed marks, allowing a slight hang. Commence at the top edge and if the swag is too long, trim it accordingly. It may be necessary to hold the swag in place with glass-headed pins until the glue is completely dry, as it is quite heavy.

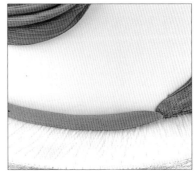

Attaching the roll around the base

9 Continue in the same way around the cake, between the marks, until the last one is entirely resting on the board overlapping the first swag at the top of the cake. This size cake will require six. To fill the gap at the base of the cake, make a thin roll of paste and attach from the end of the last swag around to where another one first touches the board. Paint it with red copper satin dusting powder and painting solution.

Shaping the swag for the top of the cake around a curve

Arranging the leaves in a semi-circle

arrange a few large holly leaves around it. Arrange some large holly leaves in a semi-circle on top of the cake and place the rest of the fruits in the centre, slotting the remaining leaves between them. Finish off the edge of the board with ribbon and glue.

10 Make one more swag, stretching it slightly to form a semi-circle around the edge of a 10cm (4in) diameter container. Use the edge of a dish, a round cutter or some other suitable object. Leave for a few minutes until it can retain the curved shape, yet still remain pliable, then attach from the end of the first swag on the edge of the cake to the centre.

Stages of making the bows

11 To make a bow, roll out the paste, texture as before and cut out a 7.5cm (3in) diameter disc. Press firmly around the edge between your forefinger and thumb to create a softer looking outline. Fold and gather across the centre, then squeeze and flatten to make a space for the knot. This will also make the bow wider. Wrap a thin strip of textured paste around the centre as a knot. Attach

one bow between the ends of each of the swags, spread and drape to cover the join. Leave the join between the swag on the board and the roll.

To make the bow on top of the cake, cut out two circles, gather and place together to make a double bow. Arrange over the end of the swag and support with small pieces of foam until it is completely dry.

12 Use the remaining marzipan to make the fruits, following the instructions given with the 'Festive marzipan wreath' cake (see page 49) to make three pears, two apples, one lemon and one orange.

13 Cut out and vein 12 large holly leaves, twist slightly and leave to dry before painting with lemon gold dusting powder and painting solution. Cut out and vein six medium-size holly leaves, paint with the gold solution and bend over the centres of the bows.

14 Dust all the fruits with silver snow dusting powder. Leave for 24 hours, then add the leaves and stalks and paint them with gold dusting powder mixed with painting solution or clear alcohol. Attach a pear on the front of the board to cover the join between the bottom swag and the roll, and

Positioning the fruit on the leaves

Helpful hints

• When cutting out the strips for the board, make sure the pattern is running across them, so that the impressed lines will be radiating out from the cake.
• Place the paste on a piece of kitchen paper (towel) while dusting to prevent the powder flying about.
• To make a stronger adhesive, mash together some sugarpaste with edible glue to a paste consistency.
• When using glass-headed pins, make sure the holes they leave can be later covered with decoration.

Holly Christmas tree

A coating of traditional royal icing and piping on this square cake is combined with edible ribbons and a novel Christmas tree to create a very festive effect.

Cake and decoration

20cm (8in) square fruit cake
28cm (11in) square cake board
Apricot jam (jelly)
1kg (2lb/6 cups) marzipan
1.5kg (2½lb/8⅓ cups) royal icing
Cream, green and red liquid food colourings
28cm (11in) square red cake board
60g (2oz) red flower paste
Lemon gold dusting powder (petal dust) [EA]
Painting solution [EA]

Special equipment

Template (see page 102)
Run-out film
Nylon piping bag and adaptor (optional)
Nos. 1, 2 and 44 piping tubes (tips)
No. 2 paintbrush
7mm (¼in) strip cutter [J]
2.5cm (1in) star cutter [TKT]

1 To avoid marking the red cake board, which will be left on show when the cake is finished, place the cake on a spare cake board while the coating is being applied.

Brush the cake with apricot jam (jelly). Roll out the marzipan and use to cover the top and sides of the cake. Leave to dry for 24 hours.

2 Colour 1kg (2lb/6⅔ cups) royal icing cream. Coat the top and sides of the cake, applying a total of three coats. Carefully smooth the edges with a sharp knife between coats.

3 When dry, carefully score around the base of the cake using a scalpel. Lift it off the spare board and place on to the red cake board.

4 Trace the pattern for the tree and the tub. Lay the tracing on a flat board, cover with run-out film and fasten down at the corners with masking tape.

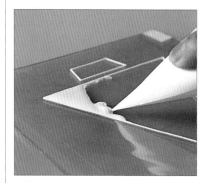

Filling in the tree outline with run-sugar

5 Paddle a small amount of the cream-coloured icing to smooth out most of the air bubbles, then place it in a paper piping bag with a No. 1 tube (tip). Outline the triangle for the tree and the tub shape, then fill in with run-sugar, making sure that all the outlines are covered.

6 Place the run-outs under a source of direct heat, such as a desk lamp, for at least 30 minutes. Then remove and finish the drying process in a warm place. If you do not need to use the lamp for another purpose, the run-outs can be left under it until they are completely dry.

7 Attach another piece of run-out film to a small board to make the separate holly leaves. Colour some royal icing green, paddle, then place in a paper piping bag with a No. 2 tube. Applying extra pressure to the bag, pipe a short, fat line, about 5mm (¼in) long. With a slightly damp, No. 2 paintbrush, pull out three points at each side of the line, dragging just the top surface of the icing. Wipe the paintbrush frequently on a clean damp cloth to remove any icing left on the tip, as this would prevent the next point of icing from pulling out cleanly.

Next, starting in the centre, drag the paintbrush lengthways along the top, in both directions, to pull out points at each end. You need to make at least 70 holly leaves in this way. Once you have mastered the technique, you can pipe more than one at a time, but do not be too ambitious, as the lines of icing soon dry and make it impossible to drag out the points. Leave in a warm place to dry.

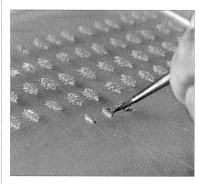

Shaping the individual holly leaves

8 Using a ruler and scriber, score a line across the base of the run-sugar tree, 5mm (¼in) from the bottom. Mark another four lines above this at 2.5cm (1in) intervals.

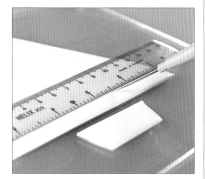

Scoring the lines on the tree using a ruler

9 Pipe garlands of holly leaves along the marked lines in the same way and to the same size as those on the run-out film. Use a paintbrush to pull them into shape and leave a few small gaps where you can add extra leaves later. Fill the triangle at the top of the tree with leaves.

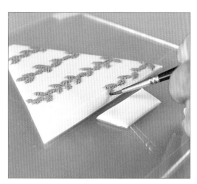

Adding the garlands of holly

10 Roll out the flower paste very thinly, and cut out four ribbons with

Cutting out and twisting the ribbons

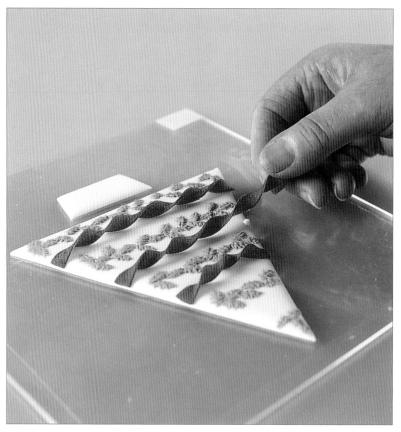

Attaching the twisted ribbons to the tree

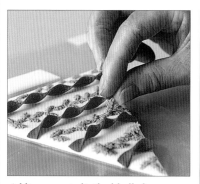

Adding extra individual holly leaves

the strip cutter. Twist each ribbon. Place them across the tree between the lines of holly. Trim, then attach with a bulb of royal icing at the ends.

11 Remove the holly leaves from the run-out film with a thin, crank-handled palette knife (metal spatula) and attach along the garlands on the tree with a small bulb of green icing. Position them to stand up at various angles. Reserve 12 leaves for the sides of the cake. Add some piped red berries, with a No. 2 tube.

12 Paint the Christmas tree tub gold using a mixture of gold dusting powder (petal dust) and painting solution or clear alcohol.

13 Mark the centre of each top edge of the cake. Cut out eight more strips of ribbon from red flower paste with the strip cutter. Twist the ribbons and attach two to each side of the cake with royal icing, slanting from each corner of the base to the centre at the top. Trim just below the top edge to allow room for piping the border.

Attaching the ribbons to the side

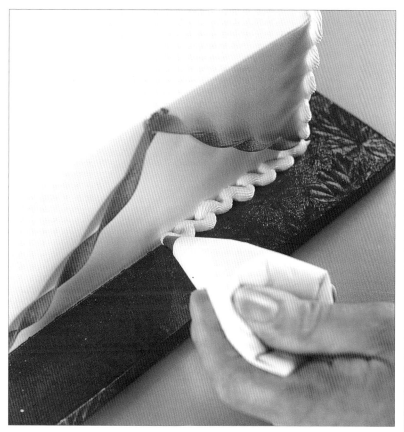

Piping 'S' scrolls around the base and down the corners

Attaching the bows and holly to the base

14 Pipe small 'S' scrolls around the base of the cake and down the four corners using a No. 44 tube. The icing needs to be at full peak consistency to achieve a good definition.

15 Trace and cut out two templates for the top of the cake. Position them 5mm (¼in) from the edge of the cake and score two straight lines down the centre edges, to form an inverted V-shape. Pipe over these lines with small 's' scrolls. Pipe a border of scrolls around the top edge of the cake.

16 Place the finished tree and tub inside the V-shape, attaching it with a few bulbs of royal icing underneath. Roll out a small amount of flower paste and cut out a star. Leave to dry, then paint gold to match the tub. Attach to the top of the cake, above the tree and between the lines of piping, by piping a tall bulb of icing to raise it to the level of the border.

17 Using a No. 2 tube, pipe straight red lines on top of the cake, about 5mm (¼in) inside the borders to form

two triangles. Leave a gap of 2.5cm (1in) at each side of the star. Pipe graduated red lines radiating from the star in the space on each side.

18 Roll out the remainder of the red flower paste and cut out five strips. Make bows for the base of the cake by folding the two ends of the strips into loops. Secure them in the centre. Attach one bow to each corner with a small bulb of royal icing. Add three holly leaves and some red berries to the centre of each one.

Make a smaller bow with the remaining strip of red flower paste and place it on top of the tree tub. Paint the tips of some of the holly leaves on the tree and on the sides of the cake with gold dusting powder.

Helpful hints

• To help you roll out the paste for the bows very thinly, smear the board sparingly with vegetable fat. Before cutting out, turn the paste over on to a surface lightly dusted with cornflour (cornstarch).
• Keep the ribbons covered with plastic while working, as they dry out very quickly and will crack when twisted.
• If you have difficulty lifting the holly leaves, try a damp paintbrush.
• Painting solution and alcohol evaporate very quickly, so mix only a small amount of paint at a time.

Piping the V-shape on top of the cake

Piping radiating lines from the star

Baubles

Unwrapping decorations for the Christmas tree is a great pleasure each year, and is the beginning of the festivities in most households. This unusual cake offers plenty of opportunity for your own innovation.

Cake and decoration

20cm (8in) round fruit cake
20cm (8in) thin hard cake board
Apricot jam (jelly)
1kg (2lb/6 cups) marzipan
1.25kg (2½lb/8⅓ cups) royal icing
Cream liquid food colouring [MF]
25cm (10in) cake board
Blue and yellow paste food colourings
Lemon gold, silver snow and mother-of-pearl dusting powders (petal dust) [EA]
Painting solution [EA]
250g (8oz/1½ cups) white sugarpaste (rolled fondant)
250g (8oz) white flower paste
Cornflour (cornstarch), for dusting
Icing (confectioners') sugar, for dusting
Edible glue
Disco coloured dusting powders [EA]
Gold and silver dragées (optional)

Special equipment

Run-out film
Nylon piping bag and adaptor (optional)
Nos. 1.5, 7 and 13 piping tubes (tips)
Extra large half ball mould [PME]
Large ball tool [J]
6cm (2½in) plain round cutter
Any small Christmas cutters e.g. star, bell and holly

1 Place the cake on the thin 20cm (8in) hard cake board and brush with apricot jam (jelly). Roll out the marzipan and use to cover the cake, covering the top and sides separately to form a sharp angle around the top edge. Make sure that the marzipan covers the edge of the thin cake board as this will remain hidden underneath. Leave the cake to dry for 24 hours.

2 Colour 750g (1½lb/5 cups) of the royal icing cream with liquid food colouring. Place the cake, with the thin board underneath, on a temporary cake board and apply three coats of icing to the top and sides of the cake.

3 Measure the depth of the cake and draw two lines on paper the same distance apart. At right angles to these and between them, draw a series of lines 2.5cm (1in) apart. This is the template for the piped pieces on the side of the cake. Place it on a flat board and cover with run-out film.

Beat the remaining icing to full peak and colour 125g (4oz/¾ cup) blue with the food paste colouring. Place in a piping bag with a No. 7 star tube (tip). Pipe straight lines, using the template as a guide, but extending the length of the icing slightly.

Piping blue lines over the template

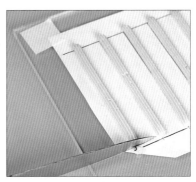

Trimming the ends of the piped pieces

4 Leave the piped pieces in a warm place for a few minutes until they have started to crust over. Using the template as a guide and a sharp knife, trim the ends. This ensures that the ends are completely flat.

5 Repeat the process with cream-coloured icing, using a No. 13 tube. When the lines are dry, pipe a random wavy line along the top of each one using a No. 1.5 tube. Paint the wavy lines gold with dusting powder (petal dust) and painting solution. You will need 32 pieces of each colour, but it is worth making a few extra ones.

6 Score around the base of the cake with a scalpel until you can lift it from the temporary board, keeping the thin board underneath. Clean and dry the board and replace the cake, leaving it free to move. Place on a turntable.

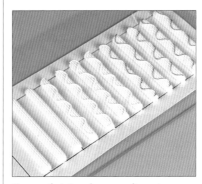

Stages of piping the cream line pieces

Attaching the blue lines to the cake

Fold a 20cm (8in) circle of greaseproof (waxed baking) paper into 32 sections. To make them easy to follow, mark each one with a pencil. Place this on top of the cake. Following the marks, attach the blue piped pieces to the side of the cake with lines of icing, making sure that each one touches the board, so that when the cake is removed, they will be level with the bottom edge.

7 Attach a cream line to the side of the cake between every pair of blue lines. Mix together the sugarpaste (rolled fondant) and flower paste and colour half of it deep blue. Set the paste aside in a plastic bag.

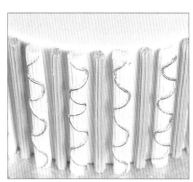

Adding the cream lines between the blue

8 For the baubles, reserve some of the remaining paste and colour small amounts yellow, turquoise and blue. Roll out a piece of the paste and cut out a 6cm (2½in) circle. Dust with cornflour (cornstarch) and icing (confectioners') sugar and gently press into the half ball mould. Smooth with a large ball tool against the mould, and press out any creases around the edge with your finger. Check that the paste is moving freely in the mould; if it sticks, remove and dust again. If you have a lot of folds that are impossible to lose, roll out the paste more thickly. Trim around the top and leave to dry. Place them upside-down on run-out film to finish drying.

Making the half balls

Fixing two half balls together

9 To make a complete bauble, hold two halves together between your fingers and pipe a line of royal icing around the join. Smooth over with a paintbrush or the tip of your finger. Leave to dry.

It is not necessary to make all the half balls into complete spheres, halves can be decorated and placed flat on top of the cake so that they appear to be emerging from a box. You will need approximately five complete and six half baubles.

Detail of the baubles on top of the cake

10 You can use your own imagination to decorate the baubles, but the complete spheres will probably need something to cover the join around the centre. A few ideas that have been used here are as follows:

Paint the surface of a turquoise half ball with edible glue and sprinkle liberally with green disco dust.

Sprinkle a blue surface with violet or hologram disco dust.

Cut out tiny holly leaves and berries and attach them all over the surface of the bauble and cover the join with a strip of green paste.

Sprinkling a half ball with disco dust

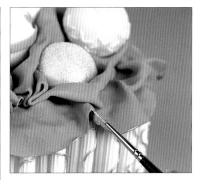

Painting the edge of the blue covering

Attach holly leaves in lines, dividing the bauble into sections, and then paint them gold.

Place blue stars on a white bauble. Place white stars on a yellow bauble and then paint them with silver snow dusting powder (petal dust).

Gold and silver dragées can be attached with a dot of royal icing.

Two half balls of different colours can be joined, then decorated with gold dragées and cut out bells.

Attach the small bell cut outs to the ball surface before painting them gold or silver.

11 To complete the decoration on top of the cake, roll out the reserved dark blue paste very thinly on a surface dusted with a little icing sugar and cut out a 25cm (10in) circle. Place this loosely over the top of the cake to resemble tissue paper, lifting it around the edge at intervals to create folds and creases.

12 Cut the rest of the rolled out dark blue paste into smaller pieces. Arrange these and the baubles, randomly and alternately on top of the cake to look like a storage container. Create folds in the paste to disguise the bottom of the half balls, and to merge between the shapes. You may need to use a small amount of edible glue to stick some pieces down.

13 Paint the edge of the paste with gold and brush on a small amount of mother-of-pearl dusting powder randomly over the blue paste on top of the cake.

14 When all the decoration is completely dry, the cake can be removed to a cake stand or placed on a gold cake board.

Helpful hints

• A nylon piping bag and adaptor are preferable to a paper bag for heavier piping. They hold much more icing and withstand the pressure needed with full peak icing.

• When you are piping with full peak icing using large tubes (tips); air bubbles can create holes, which spoil the appearance. Leave the holes until the icing is completely dry, fill a No. 1 tube with the same colour icing, then fill in the holes and smooth over with a damp paintbrush.

• To stop the ball mould rolling around while you are working on it, place it inside the top of a round cutter or suitable small container.

• When you are sprinkling with disco dust, place the bauble in the centre of a piece of greaseproof (waxed baking) paper. The excess can then be returned to the original container.

• Do not attempt to stick the circle of dark blue paste down. It is not necessary, and will make it easier to remove the whole of the top decoration before you cut the cake.

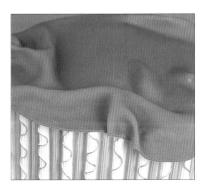

Arranging the blue covering on the cake

Arranging the baubles and extra covering

Equipment

Airbrush for spraying food colouring

Baking parchment for lining cake tins (pans)

Cake boards available as single and double thickness card, thin hardboard and 15mm (½in) thickness drums

Cake scrapers to smooth royal icing on the sides of a cake

Cake stands shapes and sizes are available to suit all cakes

Cake tins (pans) it is useful to have a variety of sizes and shapes

Clear alcohol for thinning colours and sticking sugarpaste (rolled fondant) to a marzipan covering

Cling film (plastic wrap) for wrapping paste while it is not in use to prevent it from drying out

Cornflour (cornstarch) use to dust surfaces when modelling items

Crimpers for making patterns in sugarpaste and marzipan

Cutters available in many shapes avoiding the need for templates

Cutting wheels use as a knife alternative for cutting paste

Desk lamp for drying painted work or run-out work

Dowels for supporting stacked cakes

Dragées tiny sugar balls covered in edible metallic gold and silver

Dusting powders for brushing colour on to the surface of pastes

Edible glue made from water and powdered gum, used to stick sugar pieces together

Edible varnish for adding a sheen to decorative pieces

Fine mesh sieve useful for sifting icing (confectioners') sugar before use

Firm foam sponge for thinning and shaping flower paste pieces

Foam sponge for supporting decorative pieces while drying

Food colours available as paste, liquid, jelly and powder

Greaseproof (wax baking) paper for baking and templates

Grooved non-stick board for rolling out paste to make flower petals and leaves where wiring is required

Glycerine added to royal icing for easy cutting

Gum tragacanth a firming agent to make paste set hard very quickly

Icing (confectioners') sugar for royal icing and dusting work surfaces (counters) when rolling out marzipan and other pastes

Liquid glucose adds elasticity to royal icing

Modelling tools available in many shapes for a variety of tasks

Moulds for shaping decorations

Nylon piping bag and adaptor holds piping tubes and icing for heavy piping

Painting solution mixes with dusting powder for painting

Palette knife (metal spatula) for spreading royal icing; use a crank-handled palette knife (metal spatula) for lifting run-out work

Piping bags use with a variety of tubes (tips) for piping royal icing

Plunger cutters cut out a shape and impress a design

Rolling pins large and small; white polypropylene pins are recommended

Run-out film for creating run-out and piped off pieces

Spacers roll out sugarpaste and marzipan between them for an even thickness

Sharp knife essential for making clean, accurate and straight cuts

Smoothers to smooth and shape marzipan and sugarpaste

Spare cake boards for decorating cakes on before transferring to the decorated board

Straight edge for smoothing the top of royal iced cakes

Sugar shaper for extruding pastes in different shapes

Superwhite powder makes food colourings opaque

Textured rolling pins for decorating sugarpaste surfaces

Tilting turntable makes working on the sides of a cake much easier

Veiners for impressing veins on petals and leaves

White tile for mixing colours

Tools and cutters

Manufacturers of recommended tools are listed below. The piping tubes (tips) are made by PME Sugarcraft or Bekenel.

C = Cel Products
CA = Cake Art
CCS = Celebration Cake Service
CK = Cookcraft
EA = Edable Art
FCC = Fine Cut Cutters
HH = Hawthorn Hill
HP = Holly Products
HS = House of Sugar
J = Jem Products
K = Kitbox
MF = Mary Ford
OP = Orchard Products
PC = Patchwork Cutters
PME = PME Sugarcraft
R = Renshaws
RG = Regalmarz
SF = Sugarflair
SC = Sugar Celebrations
SK = Squires Kitchen
SSS = Sparkling Sugarcraft Supplies
TKT = Tinkertech Tools
W = Wilton

Recipes

The following pages offer two different recipes for fruit cake, as many people prefer a lighter alternative to the traditional mixture. This section also includes recipes, hints and advice for making, and working with, coatings and icings.

Light fruit cake

This recipe offers a lighter alternative to the traditional rich, dark fruit cake, which is not to everybody's taste. (See the chart below for the ingredients, quantities and cooking times.)

1 Line the tin (pan), using a double thickness of baking parchment.

2 Wash the glacé cherries and quarter them. Cut the apricots and pineapple to the size of a half cherry and the ginger a little smaller.

3 Weigh the egg, add the vanilla extract and sherry and beat together. Cream together the butter and sugar, beat in the egg mixture.

4 Sieve together the flours and baking powder, fold into the mixture with the ground almonds.

5 Fold in the fruits, mixed peel and walnuts. It should be a dropping consistency.

6 Bake until golden brown and firm in the centre. Cover the larger sizes with foil if they begin to brown too much before the baking is completed. Leave in the tin for a few minutes before removing to a cooling rack. Wrap in a double layer of foil and store in a cool place.

Rich fruit cake

Most people have their own favourite recipe when it comes to rich fruit cake. My 'secret' ingredient is Grand Marnier liqueur but you can substitute it for brandy, rum or sherry.

1 Place all the dried fruit, including the peel and the cherries, in an airtight container and add the liqueur. Leave

---

Light Fruit Cake

Tin (pan) size: *All sizes are baked in a deep tin*

Round	15cm (6in)	20cm (8in)	25cm (10in)	30cm (12in)
Square	12cm (5in)	18cm (7in)	23cm (9in)	28cm (11in)

Ingredients:

Butter/margarine	150g (5oz / ⅔ cup)	275g (10oz / 1¼ cups)	450g (16oz / 2 cups)	850g (30oz / 3¾ cups)
Caster (superfine) sugar	150g (5oz / ⅔ cup)	275g (10oz / 1¼ cups)	450g (16oz / 2 cups)	850g (30oz / 3¾ cups)
Egg *	150g (5oz)	275g (10oz)	450g (16oz)	850g (30oz)
Self-raising flour	85g (3oz / ¾ cups)	175g (6oz / 1½ cups)	250g (9oz / 2¼ cups)	475g (17oz / 4¼ cups)
Strong plain (all-purpose) flour	85g (3oz)	175g (6oz / 1½ cups)	250g (9oz / 2¼ cups)	475g (17oz / 4¼ cups)
Baking powder	1.25ml (¼ tsp.)	2.5ml (½ tsp.)	4ml (¾ tsp.)	7ml (1 rounded tsp.)
Ground almonds	25g (1oz / ¼ cup)	50g (2oz / ½ cup)	110g (4oz / 1 cup)	225g (8oz / 2 cups)
Sherry	15–30ml (1–2 tbsp.)	45ml (3 tbsp.)	75ml (5 tbsp.)	90ml (6 tbsp.)
Glacé cherries	50g (2oz / ½ cup)	110g (4oz / 1 cup)	225g (8oz / 2 cups)	275g (10oz / 2½ cups)
Glacé pineapple	50g (2oz / ½ cup)	110g (4oz / 1 cup)	175g (6oz / 1½ cups)	225g (8oz / 2 cups)

Ready to eat

Dried apricots	50g (2oz / ½ cup)	110g (4oz / 1 cup)	175g (6oz / 1½ cups)	225g (8oz / 2 cups)
Mixed peel	25g (1oz / ¼ cup)	50g (2oz / ½ cup)	75g (3oz / ¾ cup)	110g (4oz / 1 cup)
Glacé ginger	25g (1oz / ¼ cup)	50g (2oz / ½ cup)	75g (3oz / ¾ cup)	110g (4oz / 1 cup)
Chopped walnuts	25g (1oz / ¼ cup)	50g (2oz / ½ cup)	110g (4oz / 1 cup)	175g (6oz / 1½ cups)
Vanilla extract	few drops	5ml (1 tsp.)	7.5ml (1½ tsp.)	10ml (2 tsp.)

Bake (approx)   1½ hrs   1¾–2 hrs   2½–2¾ hrs   3 hrs (approx)

Oven Temp.   170°C / 325°F / Gas mark 3

*Liquid egg is shown as weight, which avoids the necessity of purchasing eggs of a particular size. As a rough guide, a size 1 egg will weight approximately 2–2½oz (60–75g). Note: Crystallized pineapple and ginger can be used instead of glacé types.

for at least five days, turning the container over daily to allow the fruit to soak up all the liqueur. Prepare the tin by lining it with parchment.

2 Beat together the butter and sugar, beat in the egg. Mix together the flour, mixed spice and ground almonds, then beat lightly into the mixture. Mix in the dried fruit, place the mixture in the tin and smooth.

3 Tie a double layer of brown paper around the outside of the tin, and cover the top with a loose layer of foil. Position in the centre of the oven.

When baked, place the tin on a cooling rack, with the foil still on top. When cold, unwrap and brush with more Grand Marnier. Wrap in a double layer of foil and store in a cool place.

Note: When making different sizes and shapes, use multiples of the recipes. Measure the amount required by comparing the volume of water it holds with a round or square tin.

Sugarpaste (rolled fondant)

(makes 625g [1¼lb/3¾ cups], see p101)

1 egg white, made up from albumen powder

30ml (2 tablespoons) liquid glucose

625g (1¼lb/5 cups) icing (confectioners') sugar

white vegetable fat (optional)

1 Put the egg white and liquid glucose in a bowl. Use a warm spoon for the liquid glucose.

2 Sift the icing (confectioners') sugar into the bowl, adding a small amount little at a time. Stir until the mixture thickens.

3 Turn thoroughly on to a work surface (counter) dusted with icing (confectioners') sugar and knead the paste until soft and pliable. If the paste is dry and cracked, knead in a little vegetable fat.

4 Wrap the mixture in a plastic bag or cling film (plastic wrap) and store in an airtight container until required.

Flower paste (gum paste)

(makes 500g [1lb/3 cups])

40ml (8 teaspoons) warm water

10ml (2 teaspoons) powdered gelatine (gelatin)

500g (1lb/4 cups) icing (confectioners') sugar

20ml (4 teaspoons) gum tragacanth

10ml (2 teaspoons) liquid glucose

15g (½oz/1 tablespoon) vegetable fat

2 tablespoons plus 1 teaspoon egg white (fresh or albumen powder)

1 Measure the water into a small dish and sprinkle over the gelatine (gelatin). Leave to soak for 1 hour.

2 Sift the icing (confectioners') sugar and gum tragacanth into the bowl of an electric mixer and warm gently.

3 Dissolve the gelatine mixture over a pan of hot water, add the liquid glucose and vegetable fat, and stir until dissolved.

4 Place the bowl containing the icing sugar and gum tragacanth on the

---

Rich Fruit Cake

Tin (pan) size: *All cakes are baked in a deep tin*

Round	15cm (6in)	20cm (8in)	25cm (10in)	30cm (12in)
Square	12cm (5in)	18cm (7in)	23cm (9in)	28cm (11in)

Ingredients:

Butter/Margarine	140g (5oz / ⅔ cup)	230g (8oz / 1 cup)	370g (13oz / 1⅔ cups)	570g (20oz / 2½ cups)
Muscovado sugar	140g (5oz / ¾ cup)	230g (8oz / 1⅓ cups)	370g (13oz / 2¼ cups)	570g (20oz / 3⅓ cups)
Plain (all-purpose) flour	140g (5oz / 1¼ cups)	230g (8oz / 2 cups)	370g (13oz / 3¼ cups)	570g (20oz / 5 cups)
Egg (beaten)	140g (5oz)	230g (8oz)	370g (13oz)	570g (20oz)
Ground almonds	40g (1½oz / ⅓ cup)	55g (2oz / ½ cup)	115g (4oz / 1 cup)	175g (6oz / 1½ cups)
Currants	280g (10oz / 2 cups)	460g (16oz / 3 cups)	740g (26oz / 5 cups)	1.14kg (40oz / 8 cups)
Sultanas (golden raisins)	210g (7 oz / 1½ cups)	340g (12oz / 2½ cups)	540g (19oz / 3¾ cups)	850g (30oz / 6 cups)
Glacé cherries	40g (1½oz / ⅓ cup)	80g (2½oz / ⅔ cup)	115g (4oz / 1 cup)	175g (6oz / 1½ cups)
Mixed peel	30g (1oz / ¼ cup)	40g (1½oz / ⅓ cup)	85g (3oz / ¾ cup)	115g (4oz / 1 cup)
Mixed spice	2.5ml (½ tsp.)	5ml (1 tsp.)	7.5ml (1½ tsp.)	10ml (2 tsp.)
Grand Marnier Liqueur	45ml (1½ fl.oz)	90ml (3 fl.oz)	140ml (4½ fl.oz)	185 ml (6 fl.oz)

Note: Extra Grand Marnier should be available to brush over the cakes when they are baked.

Bake (approx)	4 hrs	6–7 hrs	8–9 hrs	10–11 hrs

For the first 2 hours on 150°C / 300°F / Gas mark 2 then
turn down to 140°C / 275°F / Gas mark 1 for the remainder of the baking time.
Test with a skewer in the centre to ensure the cake is baked through.

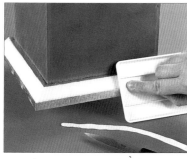

Smoothing sugarpaste (rolled fondant)

electric mixer. Add the gelatine mixture and the egg white and beat for about 5 minutes, until white and stringy.

5 Store the flower paste in a plastic bag inside an airtight container in the refrigerator for 24 hours before use. When removed, the paste will be hard. Knead it in with lightly greased hands until the paste is soft and stretchy. This type of paste can be cut into small pieces and frozen.

Pastillage

7.5ml (1½ teaspoons) powdered gelatine (gelatin)

60ml (4 tablespoons) water

2.5ml (½ teaspoon) gum tragacanth

500g (2lb/8 cups) icing (confectioners') sugar

1 Sprinkle the gelatine (gelatin) on the water and leave to soften. Sift the gum tragacanth and sugar into a mixing bowl and warm gently.

2 Dissolve the gelatine over a pan of hot water. Add the gelatine to the sugar mixture and beat on a slow speed with an electric mixer for about 3 minutes. Store in an airtight container in the refrigerator.

Modelling paste

Modelling paste is a half-and-half mix of flower paste and sugarpaste (rolled

Helpful Hint

Ideally, cakes should be left for up to 1–2 days after covering with marzipan in order to make sure they have a really firm covering.

fondant) that is useful for making paste models.

Marzipan

Most royal-iced cakes require a crisp, right-angled edge between the top and the sides. This can be created with a marzipan covering. When rolling out marzipan, use icing (confectioners') sugar to prevent the marzipan from sticking to the surface. Knead the marzipan to make it pliable and easier to roll. Use a neutral flavoured and coloured jam (jelly) to stick marzipan to the cake, such as apricot jam. (It should be boiled, and sieved before use.)

Covering round cakes with marzipan

1 Brush the cake top with boiled and sieved apricot jam (jelly).

2 Roll out a portion of marzipan between 5mm (¼in) spacers and place it on a spare cake board. Brush the top of the cake with jam and turn upside down on to the marzipan. If there is a space between the edge of the cake and the marzipan, caused by the shape of the cake, fill it in with a narrow roll of marzipan. Trim away all the excess and smooth round.

3 Measure the circumference of the cake and add on a small amount for an overlap. Knead the remaining marzipan together. Roll out between spacers and cut a strip to the measured length, adding 5mm (¼in) to the depth. If the cake is large, it is easier to cut two strips.

4 Brush the side of the cake with jam and press on the marzipan strip(s) with the cut edge flat on the board underneath. Overlap at the join and cut through both thicknesses. Pinch together the edges and smooth to a neat finish.

5 Push the excess marzipan that is sticking up over the base edge of the

cake. Place the final cake board on top and invert the two boards. Finish by smoothing round once more.

Covering square cakes with marzipan

1 Use the same method as for round cakes to cover the top of a square cake with marzipan.

2 For the sides, roll out the marzipan, between the spacers, into a rectangle just larger than the width of the cake side and four times the depth, plus 5mm (¼in). Brush the sides of the cake with jam and press on the strips, with cut edges flat on the board. Line up each piece with a corner and allow it to overlap at the other end. Trim away the excess marzipan, level with the thickness of the next side.

3 Push the excess paste at the top on to the base of the cake. Place the final cake board on top and invert the two boards. Neaten with smoothers.

Covering shaped cakes with marzipan

Cover the tops of shaped cakes, such as petal-shaped and hexagonal cakes, using the method for round cakes. Deal with corners using the square cake method.

Covering a cake with marzipan for sugarpaste (rolled fondant)

A cake that is going to be covered with sugarpaste (rolled fondant) needs rounded edges and corners. Apply the marzipan in two operations as described above, but attach the sides in a single strip. Round off the edges with a smoother or your hand.

Marzipan quantities	
30cm (12in)	2kg (4lb)
25cm (10in)	1.5kg (3lb)
20cm (8in)	1kg (2lb)
15cm (6in)	500g (1lb)
10cm (4in)	350g (12oz)

Royal icing

Royal icing is extremely versatile – it can be spread to give a flawlessly smooth top coating to fruit cakes, piped into bulbs, loops and scrolls, or thinned down into run-icing.

Making royal icing with a mixer

45g (1½oz) albumen powder

315ml (10fl.oz/1¼ cups) water

1.75kg (3½lb/14 cups) icing (confectioners') sugar, sifted

Using an electric mixer is quick and enables you to make large quantities.

1 Dissolve the albumen powder in the water, strain and measure out 315ml (10fl.oz/1¼ cups).

2 Place the liquid in a clean, mixer bowl together with the icing (confectioners') sugar, and stir.

3 Using an electric mixer set to the slowest speed, beat the mixture until the required consistency is reached.

Making royal icing by hand

30g (1oz) albumen powder

60ml (4 tablespoons) water

500g (1lb/4 cups) icing (confectioners') sugar, sifted

(Do not attempt to make more than 500g (1lb/3⅓ cups at one time.)

1 Dissolve the albumen powder in the water, then strain.

2 Place the albumen mixture in a large, clean bowl.

3 Next, gradually add the icing (confectioners') sugar, one tablespoon at a time, and beat the two together. It will take about 20 minutes for the icing to reach soft peak consistency.

Albumen (egg white) powder

Powdered egg white is recommended for making royal icing, as it complies with food safety standards and gives consistent results, which can be difficult with fresh egg whites. Being able to measure the ingredients accurately makes royal icing simple.

Albumen powders are available either as pure albumen or as an albumen substitute. Albumen substitutes are cheaper and can be used for most tasks, particularly coating, as they produce a slightly crumbly icing, which is easier to cut. Pure albumen powder is stronger. Use it for delicate designs.

Pure albumen is a deeper colour than the substitute. When mixed with water, the substitute will dissolve, but pure albumen forms a sticky mass and needs to be soaked for at least one hour to dissolve. Sieve both solutions before use.

Icing (confectioners') sugar

There are different grades of icing (confectioners') sugar available. The most suitable is known as 'bride cake' icing sugar, which is extra fine and therefore does not require sifting.

If possible, avoid using icing sugars which have had cornflour (cornstarch)

Icing consistency

Soft peak is the first consistency reached during beating and is used for coating the cake and piping with writing tubes (tips). When lifted from the bowl with a spatula, soft peak icing should retain a peak that will hold its shape, but not be stiff and over-firm.

Full peak is a stiffer, firmer consistency. When lifted from the bowl with a spatula, it leaves a definite peak, which will not fall when shaken. Use full peak icing for piping decorative borders that need to retain their shape as soon as they are piped.

Piping with royal icing

This cake is both coated and decorated with royal icing

added to them. Differing quantities are present, depending on the brand, and these icing sugars often require extra moisture to obtain the correct consistency. Icing made with this type of icing sugar also loses aeration quickly, which means that you will need to re-beat it more frequently.

Additional ingredients

Glycerine is often added to royal icing to prevent it from drying too hard, thus making it easier to cut. Add one teaspoon of glycerine to every 500g (1lb/3⅓ cups) of royal icing just before use. Never add glycerine to run-icing, as it prevents the run-outs from drying.

Electric mixer

Although it is not an essential piece of equipment, an electric mixer will save time – and effort – when you are making royal icing. Beating times vary according to the speed of the individual mixer, but you will need to beat for about five minutes to create soft peak icing and for a further two minutes to create full peak icing.

Gum tragacanth can be added to icing for piping. This is useful when making separate pieces to be added to the cake at a later stage.

Covering a cake with royal icing

Three coats of royal icing should be applied to a marzipan-covered cake. Leave the icing to dry for about eight hours between each layer. Use soft-peak icing for the first coat, then add water to soften the icing slightly for the second coat, then soften again to apply the final coat.

Top coating

Spread a little royal icing over the top of the cake (round or square) with a palette knife (metal spatula). Hold the knife horizontally and work it backwards and forwards, while turning the cake, to eliminate any air bubbles in the icing. Spread the icing evenly to the edges of the cake. Remove the cake from the turntable, and place it on the work surface. USe a damp cloth or non-slip mat underneath to prevent it from slipping. Draw a clean, straight edge or long-

bladed knife over the top of the cake in one continuous movement to create a smooth finish. Leave to dry before coating the sides of the cake.

Side coating a round cake

Place the cake on a turntable and start applying the royal icing to the side with a palette knife (metal spatula). Hold the knife vertically and position your finger down the back of the blade to apply pressure to the icing and disperse air bubbles. Rotate the cake and paddle the icing as you work to form an even thickness.

Ensure that the icing covers the cake from top to bottom and that no marzipan can be seen. Trim excess from the top edge. Use a plain cake scraper, pulling it around the cake in one even movement, while rotating the turntable. When the scraper has been pulled around the whole cake, pull it off towards yourself to finish. This will leave a 'take off' mark, which will be removed later.

Side coating a square cake

Coat the first side of a square cake in the same way as a round cake. Move the scraper along the side and, at the end of the side, pull it off towards yourself. Start the second side by bringing the 'take off' mark from the previous side around and on to the second side. Repeat this process until all four sides of the cake are coated. Always ensure that all the edges are neat before leaving to dry and applying a second or third coat.

Storing

Cover royal icing with a damp cloth while you are working to prevent a crust from forming. Store in an airtight container, with cling film (plastic wrap) on the surface. It is not necessary to keep the icing refrigerated. Re-beat the icing to its original consistency, preferably in a mixer, at least every two days.

Attractive shapes piped on run-out film make an effective and delicate decoration

Smooth any rough edges or surfaces with a sharp knife or scalpel.

Coating a cake board with royal icing

Coating cake boards can be done in two ways. The easier method is to leave the board until you have finished coating the final side of the cake. Then, while the icing is still wet, coat the board with a soft consistency of icing, resembling thick run-icing. Smooth the top with a palette knife (metal spatula), without removing any of the icing. Trim any excess icing from the edge of the board, then allow it to settle and dry.

Alternatively, for a better finish, coat the board separately from the cake. Smaller sizes of boards can be coated with icing all the way across. Larger boards should be coated with an 8cm (3in) band of icing around the edge.

Coat the cake on a temporary board, also placing a thin cake card, the same size and shape as the cake, underneath. This thin cake card should be kept under the cake when it is transferred to the final board – the card will prevent colour on the cake from staining the surrounding icing.

The cake can be removed from the temporary cake board by scoring around the base with a scalpel before gently lifting it off.

Piping with a small tube (tip)

Piping royal icing

Piping is the extrusion of royal icing from tubes (tips) to form straight and curved lines and is used in the designs of most royal-iced cakes. Tubes may be plain or made in a variety of shapes, for piping shells and other decorative edgings. First, select the size of tube that you wish to use. When piping, take care not to overfill the piping bag with icing. It is more comfortable and easier to pipe using a bag that is only about two-thirds full of icing.

Both linework piping and piping borders require accurate control of pressure against speed. However, the bag is held differently. When piping borders, you will be using a greater volume of icing with tubes (tips) of a wider aperture. Grip the bag firmly in one hand to force the icing through the tube. When piping fine linework using small tubes, hold the bag in one hand in the same way as a pen but support it with the other, which will prevent your hand from shaking and improve accuracy.

Food colourings for royal icing

A variety of food colourings is suitable for use with royal icing. The most suitable, however, is liquid colouring, which mixes in easily. The main advantage of liquid colouring is that it can be measured into the icing with a dropper. Count the number of drops of liquid colouring added to each 500g (1lb/3⅓ cups) royal icing to achieve the desired shade. This way a colour can be repeated accurately for other batches of icing, if they are required later. Paste food colourings are not recommended for use with royal icing, except for very small quantities where an accurate match of the colour is not required.

Liquid food colourings can be mixed together to produce a wide range of shades. However, blend and experiment with different colours, with some spare icing, before starting to decorate the final cake.

Sugarpaste

Commercially produced sugarpaste (rolled fondant) is high quality and available in a large variety of colours. This saves time and usually resists colour fading better than homemade paste.

Colouring

Paste colours are the most suitable for sugarpaste, but if delicate colours are required, it is possible to use liquid. Break off a small piece of the sugarpaste and add colour to this, kneading it in completely, then add small pieces of this paste to the remaining amount until the required shade is achieved.

If you add any colour directly to the bulk of paste do so sparingly, dotting it in all over the surface before kneading in the paste.

When left, the colours mature and usually deepen. Sometimes, even though the paste has been well kneaded, spots of colour appear in the paste, spoiling the appearance. For this reason it is beneficial to leave the paste for a few hours, or overnight. Then knead it again before use.

Storage

Commercially bought paste comes in special packaging in which it keeps very well. Once opened, it soon forms a crust on the outside, and a lot can be wasted by having to cut this away. Wrap any left over paste in cling fiilm (plastic wrap), place in a polythene bag and store in an airtight container.

Covering a cake

Knead the sugarpaste on a clean work surface, sprinkled with icing, (confectioners') sugar, until it is soft and pliable.

Form into a ball, flatten and roll out between spacers. These are long, flat pieces of perspex or wood, available in different thicknesses, but for sugarpaste covering the most suitable is 5mm (¼in). Place on either side of the paste and roll until the rolling pin is resting on the spacers, ensuring an even thickness.

Move the paste frequently to prevent it sticking to the surface, and if necessary sprinkle underneath with more icing sugar. If you need to sprinkle the top with icing sugar, rub it into the surface before rolling again. This prevents pockets of icing sugar from spoiling the appearance.

Brush the surface of the marzipan with clear alcohol, then lift the sugarpaste on to the cake. Stroke the top of the cake with a sugarpaste smoother in the same direction as you are laying down the paste, to expel any air that may become trapped under the top covering. Allow the paste to fall down the sides of the cake, open up any folds and ease it back on to the side of the cake for a smooth surface.

If the cake is square, cup your hand around the corner and stroke the paste upwards to prevent cracking on the corners.

Trim away the excess paste from around the base and finish with smoothers. Only use one smoother on a round cake – two will form flattened surfaces at intervals around the cake. Lastly, rub the fleshy part of your hand around the top edge. Check the surface for any imperfections and gently rub over any cracks.

Covering the board

There are two ways to cover the board.

1 Roll out the sugarpaste between 2.5mm (⅛in) spacers. For a round cake, cut a strip to fit around the board. Brush the board with water, position the strip with the cut edge against the cake, then trim the outer edge. If it is a large cake use two strips. Overlap any joins, cut through the two thicknesses and remove the excess paste. Then pinch the two edges of paste together and smooth over the surface.

For a square cake, cut four lengths the same measurement as the cake board, overlap at the corners, and cut through from the corner point of the board to the corner of the cake, then proceed as before.

2 Cover all the way across the surface with a sheet of sugarpaste, smooth and trim around the edges. If you use this method you will need to place a thin cake board, the same size and shape as the cake, underneath the cake to prevent the base from becoming sticky. This is a more expensive method as it requires a lot more sugarpaste than the previous one, but it is useful for unusual shapes where the margin of board around the cake is uneven.

Dusting the sugarpaste board covering

Templates

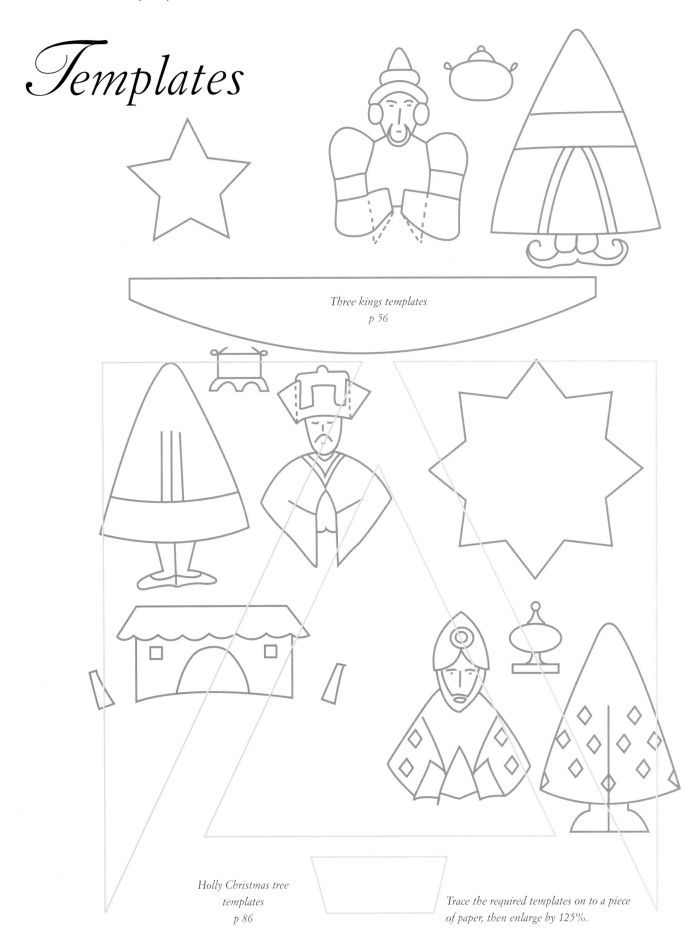

Three kings templates
p 56

Holly Christmas tree
templates
p 86

Trace the required templates on to a piece of paper, then enlarge by 125%.

*Christmas angels
templates
p 28*

*Trace the required templates on to a piece
of paper, then enlarge by 125%.*

Midnight snowflakes
templates
p 22

New England
Christmas
templates
p 18

Mistletoe ring
template
p 60

Happy Christmas
templates
p 32

Trace the required templates on to a piece
of paper, then enlarge by 125%.

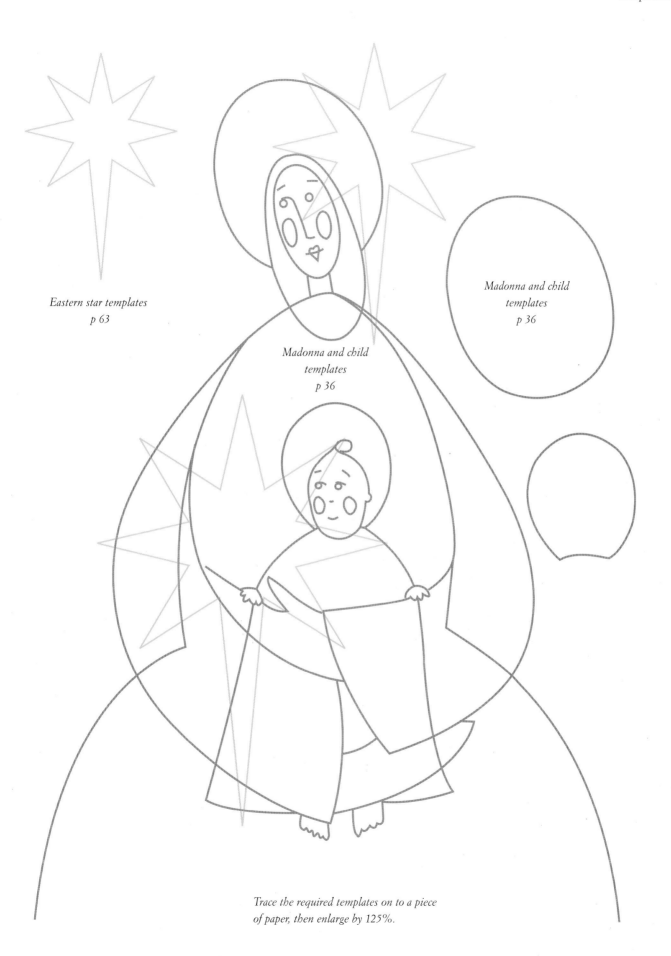

Eastern star templates
p 63

Madonna and child
templates
p 36

Madonna and child
templates
p 36

Trace the required templates on to a piece
of paper, then enlarge by 125%.

*Star of Bethlehem
template
p 66*

*Winter lace
templates
p 12*

*Winter lace
templates
p 12*

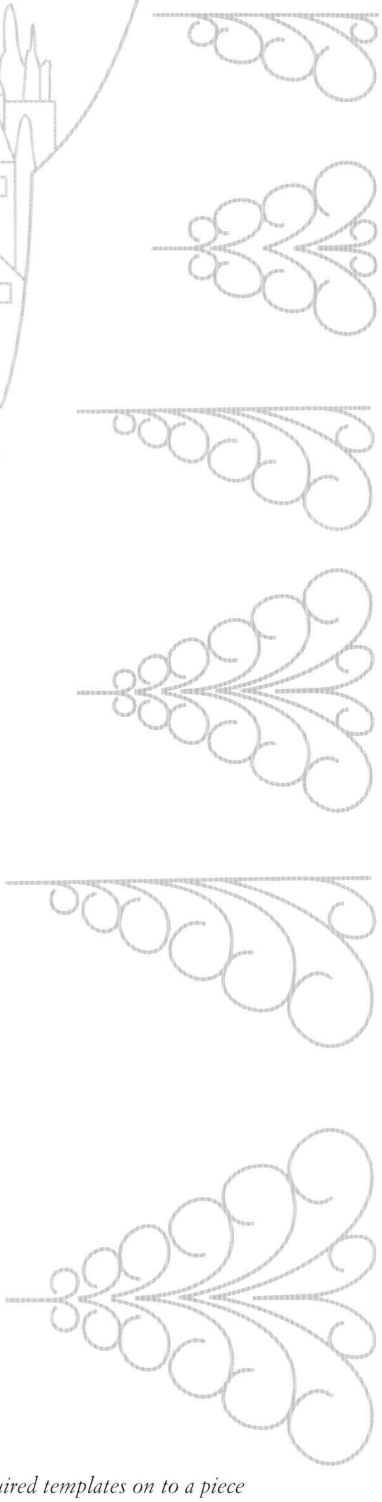

*Winter lace
templates
p 12*

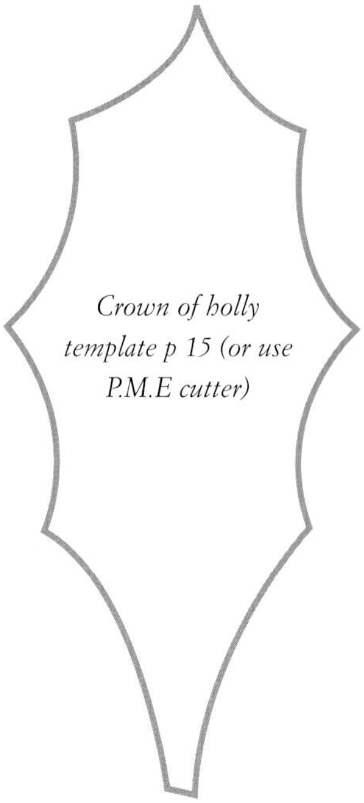

*Crown of holly
template p 15 (or use
P.M.E cutter)*

*Trace the required templates on to a piece
of paper, then enlarge by 125%.*

Partridge in a pear tree template
p 77

Nine square sparkle templates
p 52

Sparkling stars templates (Miniature Cakes) p 44

Winter berry template (Miniature Cakes) p 42

Trace the required templates on to a piece of paper, then enlarge by 125%.

Index

Suppliers

United Kingdom

Cel Products
Springfield House
Gate Helmsley
York
YO4 1NF
Tel: +44 1759 371447

Holly Products
Holly Cottage
Hassall Green
Sandbach
Cheshire
CW11 4YA
Tel: +44 1270 761403

Squires Kitchen
Squires House
3 Waverley Lane
Farnham
Surrey
GU9 8BB
Tel: +44 1252 711749

Celebration Cake Service
94 High Street
Chapmanslade
Westbury
Wiltshire
BA13 4AN
Tel: +44 1373 832640

Cornish Cakeboards
Garth-an-deys
Rose Hill
Goonhavern
Truro
Cornwall
TR4 9JT
Tel: +44 1872 572548

Culpitt Cake Art
Culpitt Ltd
Jubilee Industrial Estate
Ashington
Northumberland,
NE63 8UQ
Tel: +44 1670 814 545

Edable Art
1 Stanhope Close
The Grange
Spennymoor
Co. Durham
DL16 6LZ
Tel: +44 1388 816309

Guy, Paul and Co. Ltd
Unit B4, Foundry Way
Little End Road
Eaton Socon
Cambs,
PE19 3JH

Imaginative Icing
22 Falsgrave Road
North Yorkshire
YO11 5AT
Tel: +44 1723 378116

Imaginative Icing
21 Lendal
York, North Yorkshire
YO1 8AQ
Tel: +44 1904 654635

Kitbox
1 Fernlea Gardens
Easton-in-Gordano
Avon
BS20 0JF
Tel: +44 1275 374557

Orchard Products
51 Hallyburton road
Hove
East Sussex
BN3 7GP
Tel: +44 1273 419418

P.M.E. Sugarcraft
Brember Road
South Harrow
Middlesex
HA2 8UN
Tel: +44 20 8864 0888

Renshaw Scott Ltd
Crown Street
Liverpool
L8 RF
Tel: +44 151 706 8200

Sparkling Sugarcraft
361 Bury Old Road
Prestwich
M25 1PY
Tel: +44 161 773 3033

Sugar Celebrations
37 Farringdon Road
Swindon
SN1 5AR
Tel: +44 1793 513 549

Sugarflair Colours Ltd
Brunel Road
Manor Trading Estate
Benfleet
Essex
SS7 4PS
Tel: +44 1268 752891

Ireland

Cakes & Co.
25 Rock Hill
Blackrock Village
Co. Dublin
Tel: +353 1 283 6544

Australia
Cake and Icing Centre
651 Samford Road
Mitchelton
Queensland 4053
Tel: +61 7 3355 3443

Cake Decorators' Supplies
Shop 1, 770 George Street
Sydney 2001
Tel: +61 2 9212 4050

Finishing Touches Cake
Decorating Centre
268 Centre Road
Bentleigh
Victoria 3204
Tel: +61 3 9223 1719

Petersen's Cake Decorations
Rear 698 Beaufort Street
Mt Lawley
West Australia 6050
Tel: +61 9 9271 1692

The Cake Decorating Centre
1 Adelaide Arcade
Adelaide
South Australia 5000
Tel: +61 8 8223 1719

New Zealand
Hitchon International Ltd
220 Antiqua Street
Christchurch
Tel: (03) 365 3843

Starline Distributors Ltd
28 Jessie Street
Wellington
Tel: (04) 383 7424

USA
Beryl's Cake Decorating
& Pastry Supplies
P.O. Box 1584
N. Springfield
VA22151–0584
Tel: +1 800 488 2749

Acknowledgements

Nadene Hurst: My grateful thanks to
the following people –

Valerie Hedgethorne for kindly providing the
recipe for the Light Christmas Cake

Bev and Dave at Sparkling Sugarcraft for their help
with supplies, nothing is ever too much trouble

My friends Clare, Margery and Joyce Costello for
their help, listening ears and understanding

Cornish Cakeboards for sending cake boards

P.M.E. Sugarcraft Supplies for providing equipment

Renshaw Scott Ltd for supplying the sugarpaste

Colleagues at Merehurst Ltd for all their
efforts to produce this book

And last, but most important, my wonderful husband,
Bruce, without whom this book would have
been an impossible task.

Julie Springall: I would like to thank my husband Mikey for
all his work on the templates, his help, advice, driving and
support. My daughter Chloe, and the rest of the Springall
family. I would also like to thank Imaginative Icing for help
with sugarcraft supplies and its friendly service
(it really is an excellent shop you know!).

Christmas cracker surprise *by Nadene Hurst*
Winter lace *by Nadene Hurst*
Crown of holly *by Nadene Hurst*
New England Christmas *by Julie Springall*
Midnight snowflakes *by Nadene Hurst*
Christmas roses *by Nadene Hurst*
Christmas angels *by Julie Springall*
Happy Christmas *by Nadene Hurst*
Madonna and child *by Julie Springall*
Miniature cakes *by Nadene Hurst*
Patchwork present *by Julie Springall*
Festive marzipan wreath *by Nadene Hurst*
Nine square sparkle *by Nadene Hurst*
Three kings *by Julie Springall*
Mistletoe ring *by Nadene Hurst*
Eastern star *by Nadene Hurst*
Star of Bethlehem *by Nadene Hurst*
Yuletide slices *by Nadene Hurst*
Partridge in a pear tree *by Julie Springall*
Festive drapes *by Nadene Hurst*
Holly Christmas tree *by Nadene Hurst*
Baubles *by Nadene Hurst*

Dedicated to my dear friend Clare, who shares my Faith in God and
a large part of my life – Nadene Hurst

First published in 2000 by Merehurst Ltd,
Merehurst is a Murdoch Books (UK) Ltd imprint
Copyright © 2000 Merehurst Ltd
Photographs © Merehurst Ltd

ISBN 1 85391 833 4

Commissioning Editor: Barbara Croxford
Art Direction: Laura Jackson
Design and Editorial: Axis Design Editions Limited
Project Editor: Angela Newton
Photographer: Laurence Hudghton
Stylist: Mel Housden
CEO: Robert Oerton
Publisher: Catie Ziller
Publishing Manager: Fia Fornari
Production Manager: Lucy Byrne
Group General Manager: Mark Smith
Group CEO/Publisher: Anne Wilson

Colour separation by Colourscan, Singapore
Printed in Singapore by Tien Wah Press

Murdoch Books (UK) Ltd, Ferry House, 51–57 Lacy Road, Putney, London, SW15 1PR
Tel: +44 (0)20 8355 1480, Fax: +44 (0)20 8355 1499
Murdoch books (UK) Ltd is a subsidiary of Murdoch Magazines Pty Ltd.

Murdoch Books®, GPO Box 1203, Sydney NSW 1045, Australia
Tel: +61 (0)2 9692 2347, Fax: +61 (0)2 9692 2559
Murdoch Books® is a trademark of Murdoch Magazines Pty Ltd.